Defending Mohammad

Defending Mohammad

JUSTICE ON TRIAL

Robert E. Precht

Cornell University Press Ithaca and London

First published 2003 by Cornell University Press

Printed in the United States of America

Library of Congress Cataloging-in-Publication Data

Precht, Robert E. (Robert Edward), 1954–
  Defending Mohammad : justice on trial / Robert E. Precht.
    p. cm.
Includes bibliographical references and index.
  ISBN 0-8014-4155-2 (cloth : alk. paper)
  1. Salameh, Mohammad—Trials, litigation, etc. 2. Trials
(Terrorism)—New York (State)—New York. 3. World Trade Center bombing,
New York, N.Y., 1993. I. Title.
  KF224.S22P74 2003
  345.73'02'097471—dc21
                                2003002560

Cornell University Press strives to use environmentally responsible suppliers and materials to the fullest extent possible in the publishing of its books. Such materials include vegetable-based, low-VOC inks and acid-free papers that are recycled, totally chlorine-free, or partly composed of nonwood fibers. For further information, visit our website at www.cornellpress.cornell.edu.

Cloth printing   10 9 8 7 6 5 4 3 2 1

For my parents

Contents

Preface

Is a fair trial possible in the war on terrorism? On a snowy day, Friday, February 26, 1993, a massive car bomb nearly toppled the World Trade Center. The unthinkable had happened, an instantly recognizable American landmark had become the target of a terrorist attack.

The explosion tore out a crater in the giant underground garage, knocking out electrical and communication systems and sending waves of smoke upward through the North Tower. The conflagration devastated the busy complex and closed it for a month. Six people perished. Most of them were workers crushed by a collapsing wall as they ate lunch in a cafeteria. Thousands of other people in the building found themselves plunged into a smoky hell. With elevators shut down and the unlit hallways filling with acrid fumes, people felt their way down stairwells choked with panicked survivors. There had been terrorist acts before 1993, but the Trade Center attack was unique. These were not Americans killed on an airplane or in a foreign land. These were Americans killed on their own soil. And the scariest element may have been not the explosion, the scale of the destruction, nor even the number of dead but the sense of vulnerability ushered in by the arrival of guerilla tactics in America.

The arrest of Mohammad Salameh, an illegal Palestinian immigrant, and three other Arab men in connection with the bombing set off the first major "Muslim scare" in New York City history. It was in this atmosphere that the four defendants were indicted and stood trial for the terrorist act. I was a public defender with New York's Legal Aid Society at the time and by chance was assigned to represent the lead suspect, Salameh. The high-profile case snapped me out of my midcareer doldrums. Salameh was the ultimate underdog, and I was determined to ensure that he received a fair trial before an impartial jury. Unfortunately, the key court actors—judge, prosecutors, and defense lawyers—failed to meet this challenge.

Terrorism defendants are not predestined to receive unfair trials. If we are alert to the stress factors that can undermine impartiality, we can take measures to avoid transforming the potential for injustice into the actuality of an unfair proceeding. I hope this story suggests ways to reduce the number of unfair proceedings in the future and illustrates why, for all of their difficulties, civilian trials are superior to their most likely replacements, military commissions.

THROUGHOUT this narrative, I have quoted the participants extensively. Most of the time, my client Mohammad Salameh and I communicated in English. On occasion, we spoke through an interpreter, and I have indicated in the text when we did so. I have given Salameh's words exactly as he spoke them with one important proviso: certain of our conversations are protected by the attorney–client privilege. In a few instances, it has been necessary for me to delete portions of our conversations that are covered by the attorney–client privilege. I use ellipses to indicate deletions.

I have tried to be as accurate as possible when quoting the other participants. All quoted conversations or statements took place in my presence. Unless otherwise noted, the testimony of the witnesses, the statements of the judge, and the arguments of the lawyers during the trial are given verbatim from the trial transcript.

A considerable amount has been published about the World Trade Center bombing trial. An excellent one-volume treatment is Jim Dwyer, with David Kocieniewski, Deidre Murphy, and Peg Tyre, *Two Seconds under the World* (New York: Ballantine, 1994). In addition, Gail Appleson of Reuters, Ralph Blumenthal and Richard Bernstein of the *New York Times,* and Patti Cohen and Peg Tyre of *New York Newsday* covered the trial and wrote lively and informative articles throughout the case. I wanted, so far as possible, to tell a story based on firsthand experience. Unless noted, I have not relied on these secondary works in the preparation of this book. I cannot say, however, that they have not influenced me, for I read the accounts during and immediately after the trial, and there are doubtless unconscious echoes of them in this book.

My legal discussions of the role of the adversary system and the strains terrorism trials place on it have been much influenced by the ideas of scholars Samuel Gross and Stephan Landsman. In addition, I want to acknowledge that indispensable tool of the criminal lawyer, the *Georgetown Law Journal's Annual Survey of Criminal Procedure*. I have read and consulted this work when explaining general principles of criminal law.

MANY friends and colleagues assisted me during the preparation of this volume. Above all, I am grateful to my editor Sheri Englund for believing in this project, and for editing and shaping what I gave her into a book. I am especially thankful to Ruth Mendel, who read an early draft and provided a wealth of useful literary suggestions, and to Mitchell Berman, whose keen academic eye saved me from many embarrassments.

Thanks also to Hilary Ball, David Baum, Evan Caminker, David Forrer, Michael Fox, Kathy Gohl, Martin Gold, Ron and Lorna Greenberg, Susan Guindi, Sam Heldman, Alexis Hurley, Helen Kim, Eric Larsson, Noah Leavitt, Sandra Lee, Jeffrey Lehman, Deborah Malamud, Wayne Myers, Kelly O'Donnell, Paula Payton, Susan Butler Plum, Richard Polenberg, David Prout, Ange Romeo-Hall, Carolyn Spencer, Bonnie Tenneriello, Hitoshi Yoshida, and Sarah Zearfoss. Finally, I very much appreciate the advice and support of my agent, Kimberly Witherspoon.

With so much help, I should have written a flawless book. I haven't. I alone am responsible for the errors.

Defending Mohammad

1 My Appointment

On Friday, February 26, 1993, around six o'clock in the evening, I was late for my piano lesson. A noonday explosion at the World Trade Center had caused extensive delays throughout the subway system, and I now waited impatiently on a jammed subway platform to catch a train uptown to my teacher's studio.

The piano lessons were an escape from the world of low-level drug dealers and petty crooks I had immersed myself in as a public defender for the past twelve years. I had started the job fired with dreams of becoming the next Clarence Darrow, valiant defender of the underdog. In the beginning, I felt there was nobility in being a defense lawyer. Day in and day out, in thousands of courtrooms across the country, defense lawyers enforced the Bill of Rights, making society secure for us all. But my sense of mission had withered over the years in the face of the grim realities of the practice: a conveyor belt of small cases and broken lives, rude judges, arrogant prosecutors, and public contempt.

I missed my lesson.

Six days later, I was walking through the cathedral-like green hall of Grand Central Terminal to catch the subway to work. The scurrying commuters seemed more grim-faced than normal. They walked faster. They were quieter. I knew what they were thinking. If terrorists could strike at the Trade Center in midday, no place was safe, especially not a huge public space like Grand Central. No suspects had been arrested, no leads reported.

I exited the subway at Foley Square, a few steps from the United States Courthouse. The Depression-era skyscraper topped with a fussy golden pyramid dominated the space like a stout prison matron trying to look fashionable. I walked past coffee stands, zigzagging lawyers in blue suits, hapless citizens asking for directions to the Parking Violations Bureau, and women who spent their days on park benches. Entering our loft-like office on the top floor of a nineteenth-century building, I called out hellos to my colleagues, a mixed bag of ex–judicial clerks and veteran legal aid attorneys with hundreds of trials under their belts.

By nine-thirty I was at my desk to begin the waiting game that is the hallmark of duty days. Every one of the twelve attorneys in the office went through this ritual, twice a month. Like an emergency room physician, you wait around for the legally wounded to be brought in, for the clerk's telephone call summoning you to court to represent someone who has just been arrested. You introduce yourself to the befuddled client, make sure he understands the charges against him, and try to get him out on bail. You continue to represent the defendant in all future proceedings, unless he can scrape up the funds to hire a private lawyer. Some duty days are quiet and you don't get a single call; other days are frenzied, with many arrests, and you tend to one case after another, feeling like a character out of *M*A*S*H** doing triage.

This day passed uneventfully. By four o'clock, I was beginning to count myself lucky. Duty day would be over soon, and I would escape without too many hopeless new clients. But at four-thirty the clerk's office called and told me to come over for a credit card fraud case. At the bottom of the courthouse steps a single TV truck was raising its antennae. I ran up the steps, past the giant pillars, into the marble lobby. A guide was talking to a small group of tourists. "This is the courthouse where the Rosenberg spy trial was held in 1951."

The clerk's office was full of unfamiliar faces. A man dressed in a tweed jacket was speaking to the assistant clerk. "Can't you tell us if he's going to be arraigned tonight?"

"I don't know anything. I just work here," she said.

I entered the cramped interview room to finish the last case of the day, a young man arrested for unauthorized use of a credit card. He seemed a good candidate for bail—the dollar loss was small, and he had family ties to the area—until I realized he was an illegal immigrant. Even if I got him bail, the INS would just re-arrest him and place him in a much more crowded immigration detention facility.

"Mr. Salvador, I'm sorry to have to tell you—"

Someone was knocking on the door. I turned around. It was the assistant clerk. She opened the door.

"Rob, you're wanted on the phone."

"Mr. Salvador, I'll be right back."

I walked back to the clerk's office and picked up the phone. It was Henry DePippo, a senior prosecutor.

"Rob, we're going to need you upstairs for the bomber. In about ten minutes. The ceremonial courtroom."

I was stunned. In my experience, public defenders did not get assigned to high-profile cases, certainly not a terrorism case with major political ramifications.

The ceremonial courtroom was packed. Federal agents choked the narrow passageway between me and the front of the courtroom, and a hundred more ringed the walls. Reporters and half the prosecutor's office jammed the spectator's section, and sketch artists sat tightly together in the jury box, their large sketchbooks bobbing.

A prosecutor handed me the criminal complaint, and marshals led me through an entrance behind the judge's bench to the holding cell. When they opened the large steel door, I expected to encounter a wild-eyed zealot. But the man sitting on the bench who looked up at me appeared quite ordinary. Mohammad Salameh was small, thin, in his mid-twenties, with a closely cropped beard, large nose, and brown eyes. He looked utterly defeated.

I walked toward him. He searched my eyes as if looking for a familiar face. His expression darkened.

"Where is Michael Warren?" he asked in broken English.

"He can't be here because he might represent someone else in the case."

"I want Michael Warren."

"Well, I'll have to be your attorney tonight."

He shook his head. I stepped up to the door and yelled out that I needed a court-certified Arabic interpreter. The door opened a crack. The head marshal told me no one was available except an FBI agent. I tried to explain I needed someone who would keep my conversation with my client confidential. The marshal said it was my call but that the judge was already on the bench and getting impatient. I told him to bring me the agent-interpreter.

They let him in and closed the door. I asked him to translate the complaint and told Mr. Salameh to say nothing in response. The agent had finished the third sentence when the door cracked open again. The same marshal called out. "The judge wants to begin in five minutes."

"That's absurd, I just got here."

"Judge's orders," the marshal replied, closing the door.

"All right, Mr. Salameh," I said to him, "we don't have much time, so I'm going to summarize the charges and the interpreter will translate. The FBI traced the van that carried the bomb to you. They found a vehicle part in the wreckage and it had a number on it, and they matched it to a vehicle you rented from Ryder a week ago. Do you understand?"

He didn't seem to. In fact, he seemed utterly perplexed as to why he'd been arrested.

I re-read the complaint to see what other parts of it I should summarize to him. I noticed an interesting detail. Salameh had reported the van stolen fourteen hours before the bombing. If the van actually were stolen, he would have a real defense.

The cell door flew open with a booming sound, and eight marshals rushed in, surrounding us. "I'm not ready," I protested.

The head marshal pointed to the door. "Doesn't matter, the judge is sitting waiting for you."

We entered a hushed courtroom. Salameh was wearing handcuffs and leg irons, and he literally hopped to the defense table. The only sound in the enormous room was the scratching of the sketch artists as they frantically drew the person they had come to see. A few spectators pointed at Salameh.

Federal District Judge Richard Owen, a writer of operas in his spare time, sat behind the bench.

The Eighth Amendment of the U.S. Constitution states, "[e]xcessive bail shall not be required."[1] This important provision is based on the idea that an arrested person has not been convicted of any crime and thus is entitled to release before trial. However, courts and Congress have interpreted this provision virtually out of existence. The recently enacted Bail Reform Act allows courts to jail a suspect before trial if the government shows that no release conditions will reasonably assure the safety of the community.[2]

Judge Owen nodded. "Mr. Childers, proceed."

A thin man with sunken cheeks rose from the government's table to my left. "Your Honor, Mr. Salameh has been charged with the most serious act of terrorism ever committed on American soil." He recited the charges quietly, as if reading from a history book, but his tone was one of bottled-up anger.

The prosecutor finished. The judge looked at me and narrowed his eyes.

"You agree to detention, of course."

I hadn't had time to explain to Salameh that bail was out of the question in such a serious case. "Judge, in the circumstances, I am going to waive—"

Salameh was tugging at my sleeve. "I want for you to ask for bail."

"Please speak softly Mr. Salameh," I murmured. "Bail is completely impossible here. If you'd like—"

"Counselor," the judge interrupted.

"Yes, judge, one moment please."

I turned to my client. "Mr. Salameh, let's ask for bail later, not tonight, later."

"No, I want bail now," Salameh said.

The judge looked out at the spectators. "Counselor, I don't intend to be here all night."

I make an ill-advised bail application that may have created the false impression that Salameh had wealthy backers. *From left to right:* Assistant U.S. Attorney Gilmore Childers, Moham-mad Salameh, myself, and U.S. District Court Judge Richard Owen. © Christine Cornell. Reprinted with permission.

A crowd of reporters questions me after the bail hearing. © AP/Wide World Photos.
Reprinted with permission.

This was an important case, and I wanted to sound forceful. I embellished. "All I can tell you is that he vigorously denies his guilt, and he impressed me with his sincerity."

"He must have important financial connections if he can afford a $5 million bail. Who are they?"

I pondered this—is that what they think? Don't they know I was just pulling numbers out of my head?

"I can assure you—"

"Isn't it a little strange that he rented the van in his own name? Could he have been set up?"

The idea hadn't occurred to me, but it seemed like a splendid one under these circumstances.

"That's a distinct possibility."

I RETURNED home about eleven, the apartment surprisingly unchanged. The answering machine was blinking madly. I turned on the TV news and flipped through the channels. All the stations showed the same thing: a news conference featuring the FBI's New York chief James Fox claiming credit for the capture of Salameh; a clip of President Clinton applauding the arrest; and a shot of me standing at an odd angle against a column and proclaiming my client's innocence.

I called my sister back and assured her I was safe. I sat down on the sofa and tried to digest events. Had this day really happened? How long could I expect to hold on to the case? I finally got into bed and tried to sleep.

2 The Right to a Fair Trial

The right to a fair trial underlies a constitutional democracy, and one of the critical elements of a fair trial in a constitutional democracy is neutrality. The U.S. Supreme Court has stated, "a fair trial is one in which evidence subject to adversarial testing is presented to an impartial tribunal for resolution of issues defined in advance of the proceeding."[1] The American legal system uses a number of tools to promote neutrality. Chief among these are the jury, rules protecting the impartiality of the judge, restrictions on the presentation of inflammatory evidence, and appellate review.[2] Despite these precautions, grossly biased adjudications do occur. There are several factors that can lead to unfair trials, including publicity, the heinousness of the crime, and the status of the defendants as "outsiders." When all of these factors are present, the likelihood of unfair convictions increases.[3]

Within hours of his arrest, FBI officials began to make public statements linking Salameh to a sect of violent Muslim fundamentalists. The *New York Times* quoted an unnamed official claiming that Salameh was the follower of a blind Muslim cleric named Sheik Rahman who preached a fiery brand of Islam from a second-story mosque in Jersey City.[4] Soon, there were hundreds of published reports, fueled by anonymous official sources, that the explosion had grown out of an organized plot by Muslim fundamentalists.[5] Salameh became the symbol of a dire threat to America. *Time* magazine's cover story on March 15 was "In the Name of God." In the bombing case, the author wrote, "the arrest of a 25-year-old Muslim named Mohammed [*sic*] Salameh raised the specter that the bombing of Manhattan's World Trade Center was perhaps a terrorist act of intense cultural symbolism, framed in a religious context."[6] Politicians joined the chorus of alarm. New York Senator Alphonse D'Amato angrily charged that there was a "nest of radical fundamentalist terrorists . . . operating in the New York metropolitan area."[7] Salameh's arrest also prompted numerous threatening calls to Muslim organizations.[8]

WHEN I arrived at my office the morning after the bail hearing, the receptionist buzzed me in with a smile and pointed at my message box. Dozens of journalists wanted interviews, but no privately retained lawyer had called to replace me. She told me to go to my boss's office, where he was expecting me.

"The Feds are talking about this case in the media, so we think you should respond," Leonard Joy said. John Byrnes sat next to me, beaming. They were very different. Leonard was the Yale-educated chief of the office, sixty-three, tall and reedy with a surprisingly boyish face and a full head of hair. His attire was often threadbare. That morning he was wearing a rumpled white shirt with a frayed collar and a stained striped tie. He gave off the air of a faded aristocrat. John was second in command. A graduate of Catholic University Law School, he was fifty-one, with a round jolly face and thinning gray hair.

Leonard continued, "Larry King's producers have called, and we've booked you on his program tonight."

I soon became a minor media figure as I attacked law enforcement officials for leaking evidence and pleaded for a fair trial. Friday I was on the *Larry King Show*. The following Monday at dawn, a limousine picked me up at my apartment and whisked me to the West Side studio of ABC's *Good Morning America*. I watched the sky brighten over the East River. A second limousine drove me to the CBS studios on West 57th Street for an interview with CBS's *Morning Show*. I shared the waiting room with four-legged contestants in the New York Dog Show. A third limousine sped me to the Rockefeller Center for an appearance on the *Today Show*. I got to the office before nine.

During the next month, I gave hundreds of interviews to television, radio, and newspaper reporters. I said essentially the same thing: the law enforcement leaks were polluting the jury pool and poisoning the atmosphere needed for a fair trial.

Between media appearances, I visited my new client. His beard gave his face a severe appearance, but his sunny eyes undermined the somber tone. He was unfailingly polite. He always addressed me as Mr. Precht, but he insisted that I call him Mohammad.

Newspapers were quick to send reporters to the Middle East to interview his friends and family in an effort to uncover hints that he was the kind of person to do such a terrible act. They found few stories and returned disappointed.

He was born in Bidya in his grandmother's house in 1967, a few months after Israel captured the West Bank from Jordan in the six-day Arab-Israeli war. When he was six months old, his mother took him to Jordan, where his father, a Jordanian soldier, was stationed. Mohammad related this to me matter-of-factly. He didn't embellish the story to say that the Jews threw his family out. He volunteered that the family was not forced to leave and that he still had a number of relatives there.

The family settled in the lower-middle-class neighborhood of Zarqa, Jordan's second largest city. There, among cramped concrete shacks, Mohammad grew up with his parents and his ten younger sisters and brothers. To supplement the army pension, his father took jobs with small businesses, but the family still lived close to poverty. Friends and relatives remembered him as a quiet, respectful young man who would buy chocolates for the family.

The oldest child, Mohammad was not an academic standout. After he finished high school, he wanted to study law or medicine, but the results from his matriculation exam at the University of Jordan were not good enough for admission to those highly competitive disciplines. He ended up majoring in Islamic studies, but he was not a fanatic. He would go to the mosque to pray and fast, but his family was not fundamentalist, and he showed no signs of embracing radicalism. A newspaper report quoted an uncle in Jordan as saying that Mohammad refused to join activist groups to mount attacks on Israel.

After graduation, Mohammad faced poor job prospects in Jordan and ended up selling candy. On a lark, he applied for a tourist visa to visit the United States, and to everyone's surprise the U.S. consulate granted it. He decided to go to America to find work, as a means of helping his family. His family borrowed money to buy him a one-way ticket to New York City. It was a sad day when the family took him to the airport. A part of Mohammad didn't want to go. He was afraid he'd be lonely, but he also had dreams of a job, of money, of how he'd help his family.

The streets of New York were not kind to him. With rudimentary English-language skills, he could find only menial jobs, and after a few months he was nearly destitute. He stayed with a friend in the Bronx, but they had a falling out. Nearly penniless, he moved to Patterson, New Jersey, and then to nearby Jersey City, where he bounced around from one odd job to another.

Mohammad's tourist visa expired, and he became an illegal immigrant. He drifted into a world he didn't share with his parents. He would continue to call home once a month and ask after his brothers and sisters. He assured everyone he was well, but he became vague about addresses and jobs. His refuges were the mosque and the Islamic community center in Jersey City. Still, in our conversations, he insisted that he was not a fundamentalist. And the newspaper reporters who visited his parents' home in Jordan noted that the family did not seem especially religious.

As the month wore on, our discussions shifted to his jail conditions. Since his arrest, he had been in solitary confinement, and it became apparent to me that his mental state was deteriorating. He was confined to a tiny cell and allowed recreation for only one hour a day and none at all on weekends. Locked up, he was routinely denied the small requests granted normal prisoners, not because his jailers were being malicious but because they didn't have time to attend to him. Worn down by solitary confinement, he overreacted when he couldn't get toothpaste or make telephone calls to me. He would yell sometimes, and that behavior hardened his captors.

These confrontations seemed to sap his energy to talk to me about his defense. He pleaded with me to get him out of solitary confinement. I approached the jail authorities, but they shrugged me off. He was being kept in solitary confinement to protect himself and to protect others, they told me, and the decision was final. There was nothing I could do until the case was assigned to the presiding judge—nothing to do except complain to the press and hope that the authorities would be shamed into removing him from solitary confinement. Yet Mohammad tried to maintain his sense of humor. On our second meeting he recounted an incident that had happened the night before. After making a request to phone me and getting no response for an hour, he started banging on his cell door. The guards told him if he didn't stop, they would write up a disciplinary report charging that he tried to escape.

"That's ridiculous," Mohammad told the guards. "If I wanted to escape I wouldn't make so much noise."

We became closer, and my hopes grew that I could stay on the case. I liked Mohammad and wanted to protect him, but I had selfish motives as well. The case was a great break for my career. I now had a public stage on which to act out my fantasies of being a Super Lawyer. I no longer dreaded checking my messages in the morning, but my old anxiety that a hotshot private attorney might step in transformed itself into a new fear. As I became more invested in keeping the case, I became increasingly fearful that I would do something to anger Mohammad and he would fire me. I felt I had to keep him happy. When he fumed, I sympathized; when he suggested strategies, I agreed to pursue them; when he demanded I pay for him to have a subscription to the *New York Times*, I arranged it. I was like an insecure lover, and when Mohammad did not telephone me as he usually did, I became anxious.

He had few occasions to leave his tiny cell. His family was in Jordan, and the few friends he had in Jersey City were too scared to visit him. A meeting was arranged in the prosecutor's office, at which time Mohammad would be required to provide handwriting samples. I was to meet him there. On the appointed day, I watched as guards led him down the hallway in my direction—his face was contorted in fear. He saw me and smiled. He turned to the one of the guards and in halting English said, "When I see Mr. Precht's kind face, I know everything will be all right."

After El Sayyid Nosair was acquitted in 1991 of the main charge in the killing of radical Jewish activist Rabbi Meir Kahane, supporters celebrated in a Manhattan courthouse. The man on the right is Mohammad Salameh. © Steve Berman/*New York Times*. Reprinted with permission.

I had been on the case for a month. My client was charged with a heinous crime. He was a hated figure. Despite public and official hostility, I had established the foundation of a relationship of trust and confidence. I had no way of knowing whether I could win Mohammad's acquittal, as I did not yet know the government's evidence. At the very least, though, I wanted to ensure that he received a fair trial.

3　"We Try Cases in the Courtroom"

When the revolving drum filled with the names of all the judges stopped spinning, there was a moment of high drama as the clerk paused to read the card. "The case is assigned to Judge Kevin Duffy." I could hear muffled groans from the spectator section, but I was rather happy to hear Duffy's name. I had never had a case before him, but the attorneys in my office liked him, as he had no patience for arrogance and gave overbearing prosecutors a very hard time. He was also known for his unpredictability.

By now the case had expanded to four defendants. Nidal Ayyad had been arrested in his home in New Jersey. A naturalized U.S. citizen who worked for AlliedSignal as a chemical engineer, Ayyad was accused of ordering chemicals for the bomb. He hired a private lawyer to represent him—Atiq Ahmed, a somewhat formal Pakistani-born Muslim from Washington, D.C.

Mahmud Abouhalima was arrested in Egypt. He had worked as a taxi driver in New Jersey and fled the country soon after the bombing. He was accused of helping to manufacture and transport the bomb used in the attack. He hired Hassen Abdellah, a street-smart African American attorney from New Jersey who was also Muslim.

The fourth defendant was a young Palestinian named Ahmad Ajaj. He had been in prison for another case long before the bombing. He was accused of bringing bomb-making materials into the country that had helped the others manufacture the bomb. Because he could not afford to hire a lawyer and the federal defender's office was forbidden to represent more than one defendant in a multi-defendant case, he was appointed a lawyer from a panel of pre-certified lawyers called the Criminal Justice Act panel. The appointed lawyer was Austin Campriello, a worldly former prosecutor from New York City.

A fifth suspect and the alleged mastermind of the bombing, Ramzi Yousef, was a fugitive believed to be in Iraq. He had flown out of the country on the day of the bombing.

A week later, the parties were ordered to appear before Judge Duffy. The defense lawyers, the defendants, and the prosecutors—Gilmore Childers and Henry DePippo—waited expectantly to hear from the judge. More than any other person in the case, he would set the tone for all that would follow.

Judge Duffy was a stoop-shouldered man of about sixty, with a pleasant face and tired eyes. A graduate of Fordham Law School, he rose to become chief of the Criminal Division of the United States Attorney's Office for the Southern District of New York and then served as regional administrator for the Securities and Exchange Commission. President Nixon nominated him to the bench in 1972.

The judge peered out from the bench; his glasses perched halfway down his nose, the tip of his tongue touching his upper lip. He looked at the lawyers and seemed to fix his gaze on me.

"One of the great things about the American jury system is that we try cases in the courtroom, not in the media, and I intend to keep this tradition going," he lectured us. "There will be no more statements in the press, on TV, in radio, or any place else by either side or their agents. The next time I pick up a paper and see a quotation from any of you, you had best be prepared to have some money. The first fine will be $200. Thereafter, the fines will be squared."

I felt that Judge Duffy's ruling was unfair. Law enforcement officials had already polluted the jury pool, and now the judge was going to prevent me from responding to the leaks. "May I be heard your Honor?" I asked.

"You can say anything you want."

"Your Honor, I object to this ruling. I think it would have been entirely appropriate on the day that Mr.—"

"Mr. Precht—"

"May I be heard, your Honor?"

"The ruling has been made."

"I understand, but I want to state my objection for the record."

"Sit down, and write it out now."

In my written statement, I asked the court to modify its order so as to permit me to respond to evidence that had already been leaked by the government and to address publicly Salameh's jail conditions. I handed the paper to Judge Duffy.

He took a moment to read it. "I will grant the requests only if you will stipulate that you will have no argument whatsoever about fairness of the trial or jury selection."

"I decline to stipulate to this."

"The order then stands."

The judge moved to set a trial date.

Ordinarily, defendants must be tried within seventy days, but in complex cases the rule is relaxed.[1] Defense lawyers can ask for lengthy delays in order to review the evidence and make motions. I could have asked for a long delay, probably until the following year. I thought the delay would help the government more than it would help our defense, however, because the longer the government had to investigate, the more evidence it would find. Better to rush prosecutors to trial before they could tie up the loose ends. There might be unanswered questions the defense could exploit.

U.S. District Court Judge Kevin Thomas Duffy. © Faye Ellman.
Reprinted with permission.

I took a deep breath, stood up, and looked the judge in the eyes. Mr. Salameh insisted on a speedy trial, I proclaimed.

The judge surprised me. He granted my request and set a September trial date. He ordered that defense motions be filed in mid-June, just around the corner.

Back in the office, I debriefed Leonard, my boss. He slouched behind a desk covered with papers as if it were a dumping ground and listened as I tried to persuade him that the office should appeal the gag order. But Leonard thought the order might be a blessing in disguise.

"If you can't talk to the press, your life will be simpler."

I stuck to principle. "Leonard, the order is ridiculously broad. I can't even comment on his jail conditions."

"What more can you say about them?"

"And the fine provisions are crazy. The third violation will bring a billion dollar fine."

"They are a bit absurd."

"Leonard, we can't let him bully us like this."

He seemed to be wavering. "Okay, it's your call."

I decided to pursue the appeal, and, through contacts in my office, obtained the services of Burt Neuborne, a nationally recognized constitutional law expert, to argue my case.[2]

Meanwhile, the leaks continued despite the gag order. On April 25, the *New York Times* published a long article summarizing the status of the investigation. The article said investigators had traced nearly $100,000 wired to some of the suspects from abroad, had found links between the explosion and earlier violent incidents in the region, and had found a gas station attendant who saw Mohammad driving the van well after he reported it stolen, thus disproving his alibi defense. Much of the information was attributed to a law enforcement official who spoke on condition of anonymity.

I suspected that the source of the leaks was James Fox, director of the FBI in New York. He had called a press conference on the day of Mohammad's arrest and had taken to the airwaves afterward. The torrent of leaks that had begun on the first day of the case not only threatened to bias prospective jurors, but some of the allegations were simply untrue. Prosecutors at trial never presented the claims in the *New York Times* article that $100,000 was funneled to the defendants and that links existed between the Trade Center explosion and earlier violent incidents.

Moreover, the gag order had given law enforcement an advantage. They could get away with continuing leaks by cloaking themselves in anonymity, but the other defense lawyers and I couldn't respond unless we were prepared to pay billion dollar penalties.

I attended Neuborne's argument opposing the gag order in the court of appeals. The windows of the appellate courtroom on the seventeenth floor of the courthouse provide a panoramic view of Manhattan. It was a familiar courtroom to me. I had represented dozens of clients there on their appeals for new trials. It was bizarre to find myself in this room now, not to represent a client but to be represented by my own lawyer.

The case was called, and Neuborne stepped up to the podium. He began by reminding the court that the First Amendment generally protects a lawyer's right to make statements to the media. Although the speech of a lawyer in a trial may be subjected to some limitations, the gag order must be no broader than necessary to protect the integrity of the judicial system. The Supreme Court has ruled that a trial court may only block attorney statements having a "substantial likelihood" of prejudicing the ability to conduct a fair trial.[3] If the court wants to impose a gag order, it must make specific findings that no less restrictive alternatives exist to curb prejudicial pretrial publicity. The problem with the gag order in this case, Neuborne explained, was that the judge did not consider less restrictive alternatives.

Neuborne concluded with a lively defense of the propriety of lawyers speaking to the media about pending cases. The judicial system plays a vital role in our democracy, he argued, and the public has a legitimate interest in knowing how it operates. Public awareness and criticism have even greater value when the lawyer alleges misconduct, whether law enforcement leaks of evidence or overly harsh jail conditions. Our system grants vast power and discretion to prosecutors and judges, and publicity is the surest way to make them accountable.

The prosecutor representing Judge Duffy took his place at the podium. Defending the gag order, he took aim at Neuborne's argument that a lawyer's public statements promote accountability. The self-interest of the lawyers inevitably taints the decision to speak to the media, he argued. Personal ambition may interfere with judgment. Just as a prosecutor may hope that leaking evidence to the press or taking credit for a speedy arrest may advance the prosecutor's career, defense lawyers may hope that appearing pugnacious in public will garner them more clients. I had to admit that the allure of publicity was intoxicating. I told myself I was making statements to the media to protect my client's interests, but I also enjoyed the limelight.

The three-judge panel listened attentively, asking few questions. When the oral argument ended, I hoped the judges would rule from the bench, something they do in clear cases. To my disappointment, the chief judge said the court would take the matter under advisement.

A WEEK later, the court came down with its ruling and lifted the gag. In a sharply worded opinion, the court criticized Judge Duffy. Quoting me during my futile written attempt to get Judge Duffy to modify the order to allow me to talk about Mohammad's jail conditions, the court of appeals wrote: "There is no indication in the record that the court explored any alternatives or at all considered imposing any less broad proscriptions; indeed the court discouraged counsel from even proffering possible alternatives."[4]

In sum, the opinion did not say Judge Duffy could not enter any gag order. It said that that the one he did enter was not carefully thought out and crafted. Having gotten the gag order reversed, I began to feel like Clarence Darrow. It was my first major victory—or so I thought.

4   Discovery

I hired a Muslim investigator to interview potential witnesses in Jersey City who might be helpful in establishing Mohammad's alibi that the van was stolen from him before the explosion. The investigator went out into the field for a couple of weeks but came back empty-handed. That he hadn't found anything helpful was less disturbing than what he told me happened when he tried to speak to witnesses. "When I told them I worked for Legal Aid, they walked away. They said the FBI told them not to talk to the defense lawyers and threatened to deport them if they did."

Defendants have no general right to view the government's evidence before trial.[1] Nevertheless, Congress and the courts have established rules providing for the disclosure of a few types of evidence to protect the defendant. For example, the government must disclose evidence that is favorable to the defense.[2] In addition, certain documents and objects, such as bank records, and certain scientific test reports, such as laboratory analyses of evidence, must be disclosed.[3]

Of particular importance to a lawyer defending a terrorism case, the identity of an informant—a person who provides information to the government about a defendant—ordinarily need not be disclosed.[4] Informants range from people who are unconnected to the alleged crime—an innocent bystander who witnesses something and later tells the police—to persons who are deeply involved in the crime, for example, a co-conspirator or a government agent sent to infiltrate a terrorist cell. However, the government's ability to shield the identity of informants is not unlimited. The government must disclose an informant's identity if a court decides that the informant is a material witness or if the informant's testimony is crucial to the defense.[5]

The report from my investigator about possible witness intimidation fed my paranoia that the government was suppressing or withholding evidence. I scoured the limited discovery provided me for evidence of other government misconduct that might help our case. Something caught my eye. One of the search warrant applications contained an agent's statement that an "informant" had taught Mohammad how to drive the van just a few days before the bombing.

The existence of an informant intrigued me, and I thought it might be the key to building a defense. Was the informant a co-defendant who had started cooperating with the authorities, or was he someone already working for the government? If he was a co-defendant, I wanted to know what he had against Mohammad. Better yet, if he was not a co-defendant but rather a government employee, I might have a defense at trial. I could argue that the government "entrapped" Mohammad—encouraged him to commit the crime to the point that he should not be held responsible for it. Admittedly, this was a remote possibility. When the government entraps someone, it tries to ensure that the crime does not get committed or at least that no one is harmed. Still, the government's record of bad faith in leaking evidence and possibly scaring defense witnesses convinced me to investigate entrapment.

I needed more facts, however, before I could consider pursuing this defense. I sat down to write a motion asking Judge Duffy to compel the government to disclose the statements of Mohammad's co-defendants and the identity of the informant. I wrote my request and then looked for cases to support it, expecting to find many. To my chagrin, all the cases I found went against me. A believer in the proposition that there was at least one case to support any legal claim in the universe, I kept looking. I expanded my search for cases by looking at legal treatises, practical guides for lawyers, anything I could get my hands on. Still nothing.

I was about to give up when—bingo!—in one of the treatises I found a case that supported my request that the statements of Mohammad's co-defendants be divulged. In *U.S. v. Gallo*, a federal district court in Brooklyn had granted the defense lawyer's request for the statements of all co-conspirators, reasoning that the existence of a conspiracy made each person responsible for the statements of others.[6] The *Gallo* case was decided by another district court, so the ruling was not binding on Judge Duffy. Under the rules of precedent, district courts are only required to follow the decisions of the U.S. Supreme Court and of the court of appeals of the circuit in which the district court is located. Still, a respected judge decided *Gallo*, and I gave the case a starring role in my motion.

As to my second request, that the government be forced to disclose the informant, I found many cases that went against my position. In case after case, appellate courts ruled that district courts did not abuse their discretion by withholding the identity of informants because the appellate courts concluded that the informant's testimony would not have helped the defense. Finding nothing useful, I relied on an old Supreme Court case, *Roviaro v. United States*, in which the Court at least acknowledged the theoretical possibility that in some cases disclosure of the informant was required.[7] My research done, I filed the motion.

A week later, Judge Duffy denied my discovery motion without an opinion. I was annoyed. At least he could have written an opinion telling me why he was denying the motion. I fired off a letter to him. "I object to the summary denial of my motion and ask the Court to reconsider its ruling. The items requested are discoverable under the Federal Rules and under case law. To deny discovery of these items, especially given the disparity of investigative resources between the government and the defense, will deny Mr. Salameh a fair trial."

Weeks passed without a peep from the judge. I began to wonder whether he had ever gotten my letter. I called his chambers, and his law clerk assured me he had. Meanwhile, media exposure proved itself to be a double-edged sword. Ever since the court of appeals had lifted the gag order, I was eager to get back in the limelight and engage the media. When a producer from *Nightline* called for an interview, I leapt at the opportunity. I strode into the ABC studios near Lincoln Center filled with confidence. After all, having given hundreds of interviews already, I felt like a pro.

The producer conducted the interview on camera in her office. She asked me routine questions. No surprises. Then, wrapping up, she said she had one more question.

"Mr. Precht, we have received information that your client belonged to a gun club on Long Island and practiced military drills there. Do you have any comment?"

This question came out of left field without any warning or lead in. For the first time in an interview I was speechless. Although I had never heard of the gun club, I was not in any position to dispute my client's membership in it. The camera whirred. A truck rumbled outside. Beads of sweat formed on my forehead. How was I going to respond? Finally, I evaded the question. "I haven't seen any such evidence." I thought for sure I looked like one of those hapless victims caught in a lie by Mike Wallace on *60 Minutes*. I left the studio shaken, praying the segment would not be broadcast.

On May 18, I was sitting in my office around five o'clock in the afternoon when the call came. A law clerk in Judge Duffy's chambers was phoning to tell me that the judge had granted my motion to reconsider his earlier denial of my request but that he adhered to his original ruling. This time, however, there was a written opinion. "I've been instructed by the judge to read to you the last line of the opinion," the clerk told me. " 'I trust that in the future counsel will try to adhere to the high standards formerly demanded by the Legal Aid Society and will refrain from patently frivolous motions.'"

Feeling more miffed than alarmed, I walked over to the courthouse, picked up the opinion in a sealed envelope and walked back to office, wondering what Judge Duffy was up to now. I returned to my desk, opened the envelope, and skimmed the opinion.[8]

"My decision to deny the motion by simple endorsement, without further ado, was motivated purely by charity and efficiency. Consisting merely of a series of demands, the motion offers little or no basis whatsoever for the relief sought."

Pompous, I thought, but what should I expect? I read on.

The judge turned to my first request, disclosure of the statements of co-conspirators. Such statements did not fall within the limited class of evidence that a defendant is ordinarily entitled to, he concluded. No surprise. But the drift of the next sentence puzzled me. "One would expect, therefore, that counsel for the defendant seeking such extraordinary relief would point to some authority to support the position advocated."

But I had pointed to authority.

And indeed, the judge noted that I had relied on one case, *United States v. Gallo*, which held that the statements of co-defendants should be disclosed to the defense. "Thus, citing *Gallo*, counsel here makes the identical argument."

Then the thunderbolt.

"Unfortunately, counsel failed to complete the citation for the *Gallo* case which, had he done so, would have indicated that the Court of Appeals rejected the argument and vacated the discovery order of the district court on mandamus."

The damn case had been reversed and I had missed it! I had made the kind of mistake that would shame a first-year law student. I couldn't move. My career flashed in front of my eyes. Tomorrow morning, I would be the laughing stock of the courthouse.

Things only got worse. After skewering me on my own gaff, the judge dropped a footnote: "At this point, I feel compelled to direct counsel's attention to New York's Code of Professional responsibility . . . that . . . 'a lawyer shall not knowingly advance a claim or defense unwarranted under existing law' [or] 'knowingly make a false statement of law or fact.'" Now he was accusing me of unethical conduct. He was not obviously wrong.

Then the final indignity. The judge turned to my second claim that the government should be compelled to disclose the identity of the informant. "In support of this extraordinary request counsel points to a case which he identifies at four different places in his memorandum as *Rovario v. United States*. I believe the correct reference should be to *Roviaro v. United States*."

Yes, I had misspelled the Supreme Court case no less than four times.

Devastated, I called John Byrnes at home, hoping he would tell me that it was obvious the judge was just trying to get back at me for getting him reversed on the gag order, and everybody would see that. I read him the opinion. I explained that the book I had relied on incorrectly indicated that the *Gallo* case was still good law. John forced a laugh. He told me not to worry.

Leonard called me to his office the next morning. He sat with his hands in his pocket, looking pained. He couldn't understand how I could make such a stupid mistake, especially since I was well aware that Duffy was looking for a way to get back at me after the gag order reversal. Leonard had received inquiries from members of Legal Aid's board of directors as to whether a senior person would assist me at trial. He was now persuaded that John should try the case with me.

I left his office and tried to get on with the day. I went back to the books and tried to trace the sequence of events that led me to make the error. Whenever citing a case, a lawyer is supposed to look up the case in a book called *Shepard's* (now available on the Internet), which indicates everything that happens to the case after it is decided, including the results of appeals. That way, the lawyer makes sure that the case is still "good law," meaning that it hasn't been reversed or modified by a higher court.

In my haste to file the motion, I hadn't "shepardized" the *Gallo* case. I had found the case in a legal treatise—a kind of encyclopedia of the law—and I simply assumed the case was still good law because it appeared in what I took to be an authoritative text. Even if the treatise seemed reliable, I should have shepardized the case. I felt like an ass. I imagined all the people in the courthouse laughing at me. I had let down my colleagues and embarrassed the office.

The next morning, John poked his head in my office. "Leonard and I want to talk to you."

Leonard looked worse than the day before. He had aged ten years.

"Duffy called this morning. We just got back from a meeting with him. He thinks you intentionally misled him. He threatened to relieve the office for incompetence. He wants you removed."

"Leonard, I made a stupid mistake but the idea that I did it intentionally is crazy."

He seemed not to hear me. "One thing really impressed us," Leonard continued, "and that's how much he hates you. He thought you were arrogant in the courtroom and nasty in your letter requesting reconsideration of the motion."

I squirmed. The letter had been a little rude.

"In any case, it would be a disaster to the office if he threw us off the case for incompetence. Maybe we could get him reversed, but that's far from certain."

What's Leonard getting at? Then I had an idea about why he was so concerned. Our parent organization, the Legal Aid Society, had a contract with the federal courts in New York to provide public defender services. A committee of federal judges oversaw that contract, which they could cancel at any time. If Judge Duffy fired us for incompetence, and the decision was not reversed, the judge's committee might not renew Legal Aid's contract, putting us all out of work. Leonard looked through me. "We told Duffy you were still on the case but John would second seat you at trial."

I felt violated. Moreover, thanks to my stupidity, my office now had to think of saving its skin as much as helping me defend Mohammad. John turned to me. "Don't worry about Duffy. As long as you've got my confidence, that's all that matters."

There was nothing for me to say. I stood up to leave. Leonard shook his head. "I wish this case had never come to the office."

5 Strategy

The discovery motion was a disaster, and I had no one to blame but myself. In the grip of hubris, I had written the motion in haste, had failed to cite contrary legal authority, and had relied on bad law. The worst aspect may not have been the stupidity itself, the number of errors, or even the embarrassment. The worst aspect was that it permanently spooked my bosses. They now feared Judge Duffy and discouraged me from taking confrontational stands with him. Feeling they were looking over my shoulder, I pulled my punches. My apprehensiveness would later lead me to avoid challenging the judge when I should have objected at a crucial moment in the trial.

The next four months were a painful waiting game. I needed to file more motions, keep my client happy, and figure out a trial strategy. Yet I felt myself in the cross hairs of Judge Duffy's wrath.

The crisis prompted me to identify with my client. No, I didn't associate myself with the horrible acts he'd been accused of, but feeling vulnerable and under attack, I empathized with Mohammad. He had always felt like an outsider, even in Jordan. His earliest memory, he told me, was during the Black September massacres in 1970 when King Hussein of Jordan instituted a campaign against the Palestinians, rousting them from their houses and sending them fleeing to refugee camps. Mohammad was riding his bicycle when he saw the Jordanian soldiers searching houses. He received a gunshot wound to the leg and was taken to the hospital. He remembered, "All the walls were bloody." His only sustenance was boiled eggs and bread.

I felt closer to Mohammad, but now another person had entered our relationship—John Byrnes. He was fifty-one, down to earth, and had the easygoing manner of an Irish bartender. He had served in Vietnam and worked his whole career at the Legal Aid Society, yet he told me his childhood dream was to be an FBI agent. When John started to attend my meetings with Mohammad, I realized how limited my relationship was with my client. I had set up a bad dynamic with Mohammad. I had bonded with him, but I couldn't be candid with him. I was so desperate to please him, so eager to have him like me, so fearful that I would do something to annoy him and get myself fired that I avoided disagreeing with him. Mohammad saw through my insecurity and manipulated me by making unreasonable demands. For example, he asked me to arrange for a photographer to come to the prison to take his picture so he could send it to potential girl-friends. Mohammad was desperate to get married. He was very disappointed when I told him that I made inquires and the prison authorities said it was out of the question.

John didn't have these hang-ups. He spoke his mind and didn't hesitate to disagree with Mohammad. Far from being put off, Mohammad seemed to appreciate John's bluntness. That John was about a decade older than I may also have made a difference. Mohammad may have listened to John because he was more of a father figure. John could bring up sensitive subjects, such as whether Mohammad wanted us to approach the government and explore plea negotiations. Mohammad rebuffed the suggestion.

THERE was no death penalty statute in 1993, so Mohammad and the other defendants were not facing possible execution if they were convicted. It was not until 1994 that Congress enacted death penalty procedures and extended them to more than forty federal crimes.[1] Before 1994, the most the government could do to induce an accused terrorist to plead guilty was to promise to make a motion to the judge that would permit him to sentence the defendant to something less than the maximum sentence, which was life. This was not a huge bargaining chip. Even if the defendant cooperated, he would still be looking at a substantial sentence, and when he was released he would have to go directly into the witness protection program. The enactment of the death penalty strengthened the government's bargaining position.

After the fiasco with Judge Duffy, my boss appointed John Byrnes to serve as my "second chair." Salameh seemed to relate to him as a father figure. © Roland Thau. Reprinted with permission.

Prosecutors can now offer defendants much more if they plead guilty and cooperate: they can offer not to execute them. Is this an argument in favor of the death penalty?

As the September 11 attacks demonstrated, some terrorists desire martyrdom. The death penalty is ineffective as a deterrent and as a bargaining chip in plea negotiations. The offer not to execute such a person will not be sufficient inducement for him to plead guilty and cooperate. However, I don't believe all terrorists desire martyrdom. Some people may become involved in terrorist activities, thinking that they are playing only limited roles. When they suddenly find themselves facing the death penalty, they may be encouraged to cooperate with the government and supply useful information that could lead to the arrest of other suspected terrorists.

Conspiracy law can subject even minor players to criminal liability. Almost all terrorism indictments charge defendants with substantive crimes, such as destroying federal property, and with engaging in conspiracy or in mutual agreement to commit such offenses. Conspiracy law is the closest that Anglo-American jurisprudence comes to creating a crime of guilt by association. It encourages juries to look at a defendant not as an individual but as a representative of a larger group.

To prove conspiracy, the prosecution must show three things: that the defendant agreed with at least one other person to commit an offense; that the defendant knowingly participated in the conspiracy with the specific intent to commit the offenses that were the object of the conspiracy; and that during the existence of the conspiracy, at least one of the overt acts set forth in the indictment was committed by one or more members of the conspiracy. The level of the defendant's actual participation is immaterial.[2]

The World Trade Center indictment did not charge the defendants with conspiring to bomb the World Trade Center. Rather, it charged them with conspiring "to commit offenses against the United States," including bombing buildings in interstate commerce and transporting explosives for the purpose of bombing. The World Trade Center bombing was not listed as an object of the conspiracy but merely as

one of thirty-one overt acts alleged to have been committed in further-
ance of the conspiracy.

Consequently, because the World Trade Center bombing was not
alleged as an objective of the conspiracy, the defendants could be
guilty of the offense even though they took no specific action to bomb
the building and in fact did not intend to bomb the World Trade Center. Mohammad would be just as guilty mailing a map of the Trade
Center as driving the bomb-filled van into the building.

The government has used similar conspiracy indictments in
post–September 11 prosecutions.[3] Even minor players in a terrorism
plot can easily find themselves charged in a conspiracy indictment and
facing death. In such an instance, the death penalty might persuade
those accused to cooperate. Although minor players often don't have
terribly useful information, it is conceivable that someone might supply an evidentiary link that could help authorities apprehend higher-
ups. This is an argument in favor of the death penalty.

BACK to the case. We were definitely headed to trial, and time was
running out for filing defense motions, which were due in three weeks.
I had to decide which motions to file. There are three broad categories
of motions that determine what evidence the government may or may
not present at trial: (1) motions to suppress post-arrest statements or
confessions of a defendant on grounds that they were involuntary or
coerced; (2) motions to suppress a witness's identification of a defendant on grounds that the identification was suggested to the witness;
and (3) motions to suppress physical evidence on grounds that the evidence was seized in violation of the Fourth Amendment of the United
States Constitution. Mohammad had made no statements after his arrest, and the government had given us no indication that it intended to
introduce identification testimony against him. The government had
seized numerous items during searches and seizures, however, so
that's where I focused my attention.

The Fourth Amendment states, "The right of the people to be secure in their persons, houses, papers, and effects, against unreason-

able searches and seizures, shall not be violated, and no Warrants shall issue, but upon probable cause, supported by Oath or affirmation, and particularly describing the place to be searched, and the persons or things to be seized." To satisfy the warrant requirement, an impartial judicial officer must assess whether agents have probable cause to conduct a search.[4] As the Supreme Court stated in *Johnson v. United States*, "The point of the Fourth Amendment . . . is not that it denies law enforcement the support of the usual inferences which reasonable men draw from evidence. Its protection consists in requiring that those inferences be drawn by a neutral and detached magistrate instead of being judged by the officer engaged in the often competitive enterprise of ferreting out crime."[5] It might be added that the danger that agents will go too far is magnified to the extent that the crime under investigation is particularly threatening to the community, such as terrorism.

One of the most important searches was of a storage locker Mohammad had rented, in which chemicals were found. The FBI agent who had applied for the search warrant, Eric Pilker, told the magistrate that "bomb-making tools" were seized at Mohammad's residence on the day of his arrest. Thus, the agent claimed, there was probable cause to believe that the search of the storage locker would also turn up incriminating evidence.

In considering an agent's application for a search warrant, the magistrate relies on the factual statements and supporting affidavits of the agent making the application. A defendant may challenge the validity of the agent's affidavit by making a preliminary showing that a false statement was included in the affidavit knowingly or with reckless disregard of the truth. If a challenged statement was necessary to support probable cause for the search, the court must hold an evidentiary hearing on the matter. If, at the hearing, the defendant proves that a false statement was knowingly or recklessly included in the affidavit, any evidence seized pursuant to that warrant must be suppressed.[6]

On May 23, a man walked into my office and gave me grounds for arguing that the FBI agent Eric Pilker had included a false statement when he applied to the magistrate for a search warrant of the storage locker.

Mousab Yasin introduced himself and gave me the following information. He was an engineering professor at Hudson County Community College in Jersey City, and he lived with his mother and epileptic younger brother at 34 Kensington Avenue, Apartment 4. The address rang a bell for me. When renting the van, Mohammad had given a telephone number that belonged to someone at that address.

On the day of Mohammad's arrest, Yasin returned home to find federal agents searching the apartment. They were seizing tools, wiring, and manuals concerning antennae, circuitry, and electronic devices. Yasin told Pilker that these materials belonged to him and that he used them in his electrical studies. According to Yasin, Pilker apologized for the mistake, but he took the materials anyway.

Whether the apology was sincere or not, Pilker failed to include Yasin's explanation of the items in the affidavit in support of the search warrant, in which Pilker described the materials as "bomb-making tools." This was a serious omission, I thought, and grounds for arguing that Pilker recklessly disregarded the truth.

Yasin supplied another piece of information. On the day of the search, the agents brought Yasin's epileptic brother Abdul to their office in Newark. They interrogated him intensively but then released him. The next day, fearing his brother's arrest, Yasin bought him a ticket and placed him on a plane to Iraq. Yasin told me that the agents were now pressuring him to bring Abdul back. They were threatening to indict Abdul if he did not return. If they indicted his brother, Yasin said, Saddam Hussein would kill him to protect Iraq from U.S. retaliation for harboring him.[7]

Yasin told me he did not believe Mohammad was guilty. Mohammad had been duped by Ramzi Yousef, the mastermind. Recently arrived immigrants, he said, whose heads were still filled with propaganda against America, might be capable of such an act. But

Mohammad had been in the United States for years. He and other immigrants living here knew the issues were not so black and white, and they would not resort to violence.

I thanked Yasin for coming by. I had one question before he left. Why did Yasin fear his brother's arrest after the FBI agents released Abdul? Yasin replied that Abdul had admitted to the agents that he had taught Mohammad how to drive the yellow Ryder van. The statement sunk in. It was Abdul Yasin whose identity I had unsuccessfully sought in my discovery motion.

IN June I filed a new set of motions. I moved for an order suppressing physical evidence seized from the storage facility the government claimed Mohammad rented. In addition, at Mohammad's insistence, I asked that Judge Duffy order the Bureau of Prisons to remove him from solitary confinement, where he'd been held since the day of his arrest. Relying on a Bureau of Prisons "memorandum" setting forth the standards that would warrant keeping a pretrial detainee in solitary confinement, I argued that Salameh did not meet those standards. He was not a physical threat to other prisoners, and there was no evidence that he was in danger of being attacked by them.

A few days later, John Byrnes poked his head in my office and showed me a pink message slip left for him. The message was from Judge Duffy. The message was: "B.O.H.I.C.A." Neither John nor I knew what the cryptic message meant. One of our colleagues did a NEXIS search of the term and discovered that it was a military acronym for Bend Over Here It Comes Again. I went home mystified but alarmed.

The riddle was solved the next day. Judge Duffy issued an opinion denying my motion to remove Mohammad from solitary confinement. In a footnote, he observed that I had made another mistake in my written submission. I had relied on the 1991 revisions of the applicable Bureau of Prisons guidelines instead of the 1992 revisions. Judge Duffy did not describe the difference between the two revisions. The

1991 revisions called the Bureau of Prisons document I cited a "memorandum." The 1992 revisions called the same document an "order."

John dropped by my office a day later. He had run into Judge Duffy in the courthouse. Judge Duffy told him, "I'm going to go through Precht's papers now with a fine tooth comb. If I catch anything again, I'm going to hang him."

NEW York City steamed in July, but I froze in my over-air-conditioned office. I stared out the window a lot. Looking west, I could barely detect the Hudson River, a thin brown ribbon on the horizon. Between the river and me were other low-rise nineteenth-century cast-iron buildings of Tribeca, a rare sight in a city dominated by skyscrapers. On top of many buildings were massive air-conditioning units that spewed a neon green coolant into large open vats in an endless stream.

For my part, I was receiving an endless stream of discovery. The boxes kept coming, and much of their contents was inscrutable. There were boxes of bank records, telephone bills, transcripts of tape recordings that never mentioned my client, boxes of immigration documents with names I had never heard of, airplane tickets, residential leases, and hospital records. Then the boxes of scientific reports began to arrive, some days five at a time. I didn't know the significance of all these materials or how the government planned to use them, but their sheer volume alarmed me. The thought crossed my mind that the government was simply deluging me with a lot of irrelevant evidence to conceal what was relevant, knowing that I could never sift through all the documents before trial.

One document piqued my interest. It was a scientific report from the FBI's famous crime laboratory in Washington, D.C. The report claimed that urea nitrate—a rare explosive—had been found on a tire fragment discovered in the bomb crater. If true, this was damaging evidence. During the search of the storage locker Mohammad had rented, investigators found traces of urea nitrate.

I retained a bomb expert based in England, John Lloyd, to look at the report and analyze the government's other chemical data. Within days, Dr. Lloyd faxed me his analysis. He immediately discovered a discrepancy. The instrumental data quoted in the FBI report that supposedly demonstrated the presence of the explosive urea nitrate on the tire fragment actually showed only the presence of urea and nitric acid, two naturally occurring substances that could have come from common sources such as exhaust fumes or urine. There was no basis for the report's conclusion that the tire fragment had traces of urea nitrate. In fact, according Lloyd, as a result of the contamination at the blast site from ruptured pipes, the precise contents of the bomb could never be pinpointed.

A few weeks later, the government sent me a revised lab report retracting the earlier assertion that urea nitrate had been found. I asked Dr. Lloyd if the FBI could have made an honest mistake in the earlier report. "I can't explain how any competent chemist could produce those findings," he said.

Meanwhile, Mohammad was deteriorating in jail. Worried, cut off from friends and family, and confined to a cinder block cage, he had become overwhelmed with the maddening indignities of prison life. In solitary confinement, he and his co-defendants were not allowed access to the small diversions other prisoners enjoyed—no television, no socializing, and no freedom to do routine tasks such as washing clothes. He took out his anger on the guards, and they reacted by clamping down harder on him—if that were possible—by denying him phone calls and newspapers. He had nothing to do but brood.

Mohammad demanded to see me every day but refused to talk to me about the case. He would only complain about his jail conditions. The authorities were doing this to him intentionally, he said, trying to wear him down and make him go mad. If I didn't make the issue a cause celebre with the press, he'd fire me. I tried my best to calm Mohammad and avoided talking to the press because I thought they would be unsympathetic. Mohammad would always regain his senses and apologize—"Please give me excuse. I am very nervous"—but the issue of his jail conditions didn't go away and would surface again and again, sometimes with great disruptive force as the trial progressed. It was a constant headache.

August. Crickets droned in City Hall Park. The boxes of discovery now blocked the window so I could no longer stare out at the city. My office resembled an Egyptian tomb. A mixture of boredom and helplessness descended on me. I wanted the trial to start. I imagined scenarios of being removed from the case at the last moment.

John and I struggled to settle on a defense theory, but the ground was shifting beneath us. In the second weekend of August, we holed up in the office—crunch time. First, we reviewed the state of our own investigation. Unfortunately, our investigator had found no helpful witnesses. Whether this was because none existed or because potential witnesses felt too scared to talk to us, we could not be sure, but we realized that we were unlikely to have witnesses to call after the government rested. Hence, we needed to cobble together a defense from the government's own evidence.

We reviewed the options. Should we claim Mohammad had nothing to do with the plot? It would never work. There was too much evidence tying Mohammad to key locations. Should we argue that the U.S. government engineered the bombing? Why would it? Ridiculous. Could we blame the Israelis somehow, arguing that they set this up to discredit Arabs in America? But why would they run the risk of being caught? What about the Egyptians? Same problem. And if none of these was a plausible option, what was left?

"We'll have to work with what we've got," John said. "Our best piece of evidence is the fact that Mohammad reported the van stolen before the explosion. He also rented it in his own name. Why would anyone do that? He had to have been set up."

"By whom?"

"It doesn't matter at this point. Probably Ramzi Yousef, because he lived with our guy. But we should wait to see what happens at trial."

This strategy had one great advantage going for it. If we argued that Mohammad was duped, we could concede much of the government's evidence. If Yousef or someone else manipulated him into believing what he was doing was proper, Mohammad's presence at the storage locker and at the house in Jersey City linked to explosives could have been innocent. If someone duped him, he could have rented the van innocently. The critical battleground for us would be Mohammad's alibi. If the government couldn't prove that Mohammad lied when he reported the van stolen, the dupe theory might hold water. If it could, the defense theory was sunk.

But just as John and I thought we had agreed on a defense strategy, a new development sent us into a tailspin. Had we totally misjudged the case? On August 25, less than three weeks before the beginning of jury selection, a federal grand jury in Manhattan indicted a radical Muslim, Sheik Omar Rahman, for allegedly leading a "war of urban terrorism" that included the bombing of the World Trade Center as well as foiled plots to blow up other New York City landmarks. The alleged "organization," as it was described in the indictment, was formed at least four years earlier and was responsible for the 1990 assassination of the ultra-right Rabbi Meir Kahane, a U.S. citizen who had preached hatred against Arabs.

Fifteen suspects, including the sheik, were charged as defendants in the conspiracy. Curiously, the four Trade Center defendants were described as followers of the sheik and named as unindicted coconspirators. In other words, they were deemed to be involved in this grand scheme. Yet they were not formally charged, presumably because they had been separately charged in the case about to go to trial. The fifty-five-year-old blind sheik had headed the mosque for several years. According to the indictment, his sermons denouncing the secular Egyptian government and allegedly urging holy war were the ideological basis of the terrorist acts committed by his followers, including our defendants. The sheik was placed in the same cell block as Mohammad to await trial.

The new case was based on the work of a shadowy confidential informant named Emad Salem. A former Egyptian army colonel, Salem was recruited by the FBI to spy on members of the Jersey City Arabic community after the Kahane assassination. Salem infiltrated the mosque, became a close aide of the sheik, and secretly tape-recorded hundreds of hours of conversations between himself and the alleged plotters, including the sheik. To the dismay of his FBI handlers, he also secretly recorded conversations between himself and his handlers.

The defendants in the new case were represented by William Kunstler, one of the country's most outrageous and effective defense lawyers. Kunstler had gained fame in the 1960s defending Vietnam War protesters. His most famous case during this period was the trial of the Chicago Seven, in which he represented radicals accused of conspiring to riot during the 1968 Democratic National Convention. He baited the federal judge trying the case. He complained loudly that the judge was favoring the prosecution in his rulings. Among his antics, Kunstler boasted that his entry in *Who's Who* was longer than the judge's, exclaimed how ashamed he was to be an American lawyer, and challenged the judge to hold him in contempt. Soon the trial resembled a circus. The defendants snacked in court, tried to hold a birthday party, and hurled insults at the judge. Later in his career, Kunstler defended Native American and Black Panther activists. His defenses in all these cases were some variation of the argument that the U.S. government was responsible for the crimes. True to form, Kunstler was quick to blame Emad Salem. He told reporters that the secretly recorded tapes would contain evidence that Salem had entrapped the defendants.

The sheik's case unleashed a new wave of publicity. Newspaper headlines described the case as the "Plot to Blow Up New York." The targets of the alleged plot included the United Nations building and the Holland Tunnel. The media speculated wildly about what the carnage would have been if the plot had succeeded. Moreover, the fact that fifteen suspects had been arrested added to the aura that New York was under siege. With the trial starting soon and with fresh media reports linking Mohammad and the others to this plot, John and I concluded that a fair trial would be impossible in New York. We hired a jury expert and enlisted the help of Mark Gombiner, an appellate lawyer in our office, to draft a motion for a change of venue.

John and I were confused by the new case. Based on the discovery material, I expected the government to argue in the coming trial that Ramzi Yousef was the mastermind, not Sheik Rahman. From what I could tell, Mohammad and the others did not revere the sheik. Quite the opposite—they poked fun at him. Mohammad laughingly described to me Abouhalima's comical impression of the sheik in jail. Pretending to be the sheik, Abouhalima rolls his unseeing eyes backward, lifts his arms, and starts to sing the melody for calling the faithful to prayer. But in the routine Abouhalima changes the words and the sheik calls his jailers for a shower. In short, these were not people who would risk their necks for the sheik, but it now appeared that the government would be arguing in the second case that the sheik was the mastermind. How could the government have it both ways? The secretly recorded tapes of the informant, Emad Salem, also presented intriguing possibilities. Did Salem record any conversations with his FBI handlers that might help our defense? As Kunstler speculated, did Salem say anything that suggested he had entrapped Mohammad and the others? We didn't have time to think deeply about the implications. The new case was just one jagged piece in a puzzle that seemed to be growing every day.

We filed our new motions. We asked Judge Duffy to move the trial to another city on the grounds that the government's pretrial leaks and the new case involving the sheik made it impossible for Mohammad to get a fair trial in New York City. In the alternative, we asked the judge to require prospective jurors to complete written questionnaires before he interviewed them personally. We believed that prospective jurors would be more candid and reveal more personal information in response to sensitive questions if they completed a self-administered written questionnaire than if they were queried in the public and unfamiliar setting of the courtroom.[8] We attached a proposed questionnaire with the motion; it probed potential jurors on such topics as the role of Muslim women, donations to Israel, and Hollywood's portrayal of Arabs.

Six months earlier I had argued strenuously for a speedy trial. But with August drawing to a close and the trial imminent, it was now painfully clear that John and I hadn't had enough time to digest all the evidence or to stand far enough back from it to get a perspective. We didn't know how all the pieces fit together. We had one consolation, though. Neither did the prosecutors.

---

6 "Can You Be Fair and Impartial?"

Most crimes receive little attention from the media. A few, however, are heavily publicized, and recently the most heavily publicized crimes have been terrorist acts. In terrorism cases, most if not all jurors will have heard all sorts of things about the case before they get to court, many of which are false, inflammatory, and inadmissible. The jurors probably will share a general state of communal outrage. All of this makes them more likely to convict the defendants. Courts have tools to reduce the impact of pretrial publicity. Judge Duffy declined to use some important ones.

The day before jury selection was to begin, Judge Duffy denied all my motions. Most notably, he denied my motion for a change of venue. The judge ruled that the publicity engendered by the World Trade Center explosion was so widespread that there was no place where the case could be more fairly tried than in New York City. He added:

Counsel for Salameh points a finger at the Government for this state of affairs. The fault, as counsel knows full well, however, does not lie with the Government. This court attempted to prevent the dissemination of prejudicial publicity by imposing a "gag order" upon the attorneys and their agents at the time the matter initially came before me. Counsel for Salameh strenuously objected to this order, and successfully had it vacated by the Court of Appeals. In effect, counsel is really complaining that he was unable to "control" the publicity.

Judge Duffy also rejected my request that he use a written questionnaire when he interviewed prospective jurors. "There has been . . . absolutely no showing that jury questionnaires are of any particular help in the selection of a jury in highly publicized cases where a searching voir dire is conducted."[1]

The next morning, September 15, the jury selection process began. The clerk's office had sent juror summonses in July to thousands of people in New York City and neighboring counties. Those who responded were now assembled in a waiting room two floors below the courtroom.

Judge Duffy took the bench and started the first phase of the selection process. Potential jurors were sent to the courtroom in groups of fifty. Judge Duffy first introduced the defendants. As he called out Abouhalima, the taxi driver, Ayyad, the chemical engineer, and Ajaj, the jailed Palestinian, each young man stood up in a suit, turned with somber expressions to face the prospective jurors, and bowed slightly. When he called out Mohammad's name, Mohammad stood up in his blue prison uniform, turned, and flashed a toothy smile. At the last moment, he had rejected the idea of wearing the suit my office had provided on the grounds that it did not fit well.

After introducing the defendants, the judge introduced the lawyers. "The lead attorney for the government is Mr. Gilmore Childers." A tall, thin man of thirty-eight stood up and faced the spectator section filled with prospective jurors. Childers had an unpretentious manner that somehow reminded me of a midwestern farmer. He was different from most of the attorneys in the Southern District. They tended to come from elite backgrounds—a famous law school, followed by a prestigious judicial clerkship. Childers was a career prosecutor. A graduate of Boston College Law School, he had worked for years as an assistant district attorney in Brooklyn before moving across the river in 1988 to work for the Feds. I liked him. Straight as an arrow but able to laugh at himself. Judge Duffy introduced Childers's co-counsel, Henry DePippo. DePippo, thirty-three, a graduate of Georgetown University Law School, had worked in a law firm before becoming a federal prosecutor. He was more tightly wound than Childers, with a haughty, biting manner.

"OK, now I want to introduce the defense lawyers," Judge Duffy said. "The attorneys for Mr. Salameh, Bobby Precht and John Byrnes."

Bobby?

"Will you stand up? Anybody know either of these two gentlemen? No, OK."

He introduced Atiq Ahmed, the attorney for Nidal Ayyad, the naturalized U.S. citizen accused of ordering chemicals and sending a letter claiming responsibility for the bombing. Ahmed, thirty-eight, was polite and soft-spoken. Born in Pakistan, he moved to the United States in the 1970s, graduated from Georgetown, and went into solo practice in Washington, D.C., trying low-level criminal cases.

Next, Judge Duffy introduced Hassen Abdellah, attorney for Mahmud Abouhalima, an Egyptian-born taxi cab driver accused of helping to construct the bomb. A handsome, trim African American man of thirty-five rose, faced the spectators, and muttered a greeting in Arabic. Abdellah had the looks and charisma of a superstar. A self-made man, he had grown up in Elizabeth, New Jersey, won a football scholarship to Bucknell University, and went to Seton Hall Law School. After a six-year hitch with the Union County prosecutor's office, he went into private practice. He had won lots of acquittals in front of mostly black juries. This case was his first in federal court.

Finally, Judge Duffy introduced Austin Campriello, the attorney for Ajaj, the defendant accused of bringing bomb manuals into the country. Campriello was forty-seven, owlish, and had a smart-alecky manner. The most establishment-oriented lawyer of the group, he was then serv-

The out-of-towners. Defense attorneys Atiq Ahmed (*left*) and Hassen Abdellah. © Faye Ellman. Reprinted with permission.

ing as president of the New York Criminal Bar Association. A graduate of Columbia Law School and former chief of the Rackets Bureau of the New York County district attorney's office, he was now in private practice specializing in defending white-collar criminals.

The introductions over, the judge recessed for lunch. It had been an embarrassing morning. Whereas his co-defendants had taken care to look like three well-dressed college kids, Mohammad had flaunted the fact that he was a jailbird. He not only stuck out but he detracted from the overall image of respectability that his co-defendants wished to present as a group. And his defiance suggested that I didn't have control over him.

As John and I left the courtroom, Abdellah came up to us. I knew he was unhappy that Mohammad had not come in a suit, but I was in no mood to talk to him.

"Did you ask Mohammad whether he wanted to wear a traditional Islamic suit?"

What the hell was he talking about? I wished he would get lost. "No."

Abdellah persisted. "I don't want to tell you guys what to do but—" John shot back, "Don't."

After lunch, Judge Duffy explained the charges and entertained requests from those who sought to be excused from jury service because they were friends or associates of any of the participants or had close relatives in law enforcement. By this time, approximately 60 out of 150 possible jurors remained. The court recessed for the day.

The next morning, Judge Duffy began the second stage of jury selection. He placed jurors in five groups of twelve. Each group was brought separately into open court, where the judge asked a series of questions, including "Have you ever had an incident in your life that would make it difficult to judge another person because of their race or creed or national origin or anything like that?" and "Do you think you could be fair and impartial in a case like this?" Jurors who believed that they would have difficulty judging the case were invited into the robing room to explain their reasons to the judge and the lawyers.

Defense attorneys Austin Campriello (*left*) and Hassen Abdellah confer in Foley Square outside the courthouse. © Keith Meyers/*New York Times*. Reprinted with permission.

Some people offered absurd excuses as to why they shouldn't have to serve on the jury. Judge Duffy dismissed these people with contempt. When an investment banker at Merrill Lynch sought dismissal because some of his clients worked in the Trade Center, Judge Duffy snapped, "I'll tell Steve Hammerman exactly what a wonderful citizen you are. Good-bye. Do you know who Mr. Hammerman is?"

"Mr. Hammerman? I'm sorry. No, I do not."

"Well, you should. He's vice-chairman of the board of Merrill Lynch. Good-bye."

A Wall Street broker pleaded that serving on the jury for several months would hurt his career. Judge Duffy looked at him coldly. "If I possibly could, I'd lift your license and put you back out on the street. Go ahead. The next time somebody from your firm is accused of securities violations, I hope that none of his peers sits on his jury."

The other people who sought to be relieved from serving on the jury expressed concern that they could not be impartial. Judge Duffy dismissed these people as well, but not without gently chiding them about their civic duty. When a middle-aged woman who cared for elderly people expressed concern that jury service would aggravate her asthma, Judge Duffy took her hand. "Hold my hand, all right? What do you feel?"

"Warm."

"Okay. Every one of those guys, everybody in this room is a human being just like the human beings you care for, just like yourself, all right?"

"Yeah."

A woman said she couldn't be impartial because she had a friend who was working in a building near the Trade Center when the explosion occurred. The judge replied: "Let me suggest to you the following: suppose, instead of arresting the four guys who are outside, the FBI arrested your friend because they knew that your friend was on Vesey Street and knew exactly all about her movements and how she was seen leaving the Trade Center. Suppose the FBI said your friend was responsible for blowing the Trade Center up. Would you think that people should duck jury service if your friend was here on trial?"

"Well—"

The third stage of jury selection began. Judge Duffy questioned each remaining potential juror privately in the jury room, with all the lawyers present. One of the primary aims of these interviews was to determine if the publicity before trial had made it impossible for the jurors to be impartial.

While pretrial publicity can prejudice jurors and violate a defendant's right to an impartial jury, the constitutional requirement of impartiality does not mean that only persons completely ignorant of the facts of a case may serve on the jury. The question the trial judge must answer is whether the publicity has so hardened their opinions that they cannot impartially judge the defendant's guilt. Jurors must be able to put aside beliefs shaped by what they learned from the media and render a verdict based solely on the evidence presented in the courtroom.[1]

Judge Duffy sat at the head of a long wood table, and the lawyers sat on either side. The jurors were asked to come to the robing room one at a time and then were directed by Judge Duffy to sit next to him. He asked each a series of questions to test their attitudes about the case. He then excused the juror briefly and entertained requests from the lawyers for follow-up questions or arguments as to why the juror should be removed for cause.

Some of the most important questions that Judge Duffy asked were in the form of leading questions that suggested a "right" answer. For example, he asked prospective jurors, "Do you have any strong feelings against the United States government, the Department of Justice, the U.S. attorney's office, FBI, Secret Service, Customs?" He asked, "Do you hold any views which would prevent you from judging someone because he's a member of the Islamic faith?" The structure of the questions suggested that these were negative attitudes and should be avoided. Perhaps not surprisingly, most of the jurors answered "no" and were then released to become part of the final jury pool from which the actual jury members would be picked.

Occasionally, jurors would be removed for cause, that is, because they gave answers that indicated they could not be fair or could not serve for other reasons. Childers asked Judge Duffy to remove a potential juror for cause because the juror had been observed frequently talking to himself in the courtroom. "What I'm afraid of, judge," Childers said, "is that we get a note during deliberations that says, "We're deadlocked 11 to 2." Judge Duffy removed the juror for cause. At the request of the defense, he removed for cause a juror who said that he would be more likely to believe a government chemist than he would a defense chemist.

On one occasion, a juror who said she could be fair still asked to be excused. She was a well-dressed woman in her fifties. She seemed disappointed with herself. "I believe that I could be fair and impartial. I believe, however, as I have listened to the religious preferences of the people who have been on this panel that I am the first person who is Jewish. I don't think that my anonymity could be preserved. And so after much thought, and I agree with you that if our judicial system is to work, people must be willing to serve, but I think under these circumstances that I am not willing to be on the jury."

Judge Duffy looked at her tenderly. "Understandable. Understandable." Lying slightly, he added, "I never ask the reason why."

As she walked to the door, Abdellah called out. "It would have been an honor to have you on our panel, ma'am." This juror was an exception. The majority of prospective jurors who were questioned by Judge Duffy moved to the final pool.

In the second week of interviews, Mohammad refused to come to court. He told us he wanted to speak to the judge. We asked Duffy if he'd see Mohammad and he agreed. Three marshals led Mohammad into the robing room in handcuffs. The judge sat behind a bare desk. An interpreter was present. Mohammad bowed. "Good afternoon. I will be able to express myself better in Arabic."

"Yes, absolutely."

"In the name of God, the merciful, compassionate, at the beginning I would like to explain to you the circumstances under which I am living in prison. I am in MCC unit Nine South. And these are individual solitary confinement cells. It is a very small cell, seven by eight feet, and it is the place I sleep in and it is the place where the toilet is."

He described his ordeal from the day of his arrest to the present. He complained that the jail authorities treated him more harshly than they did other inmates. In the first month, they granted him no recreation at all, except for the one hour he met with me. During those meetings, they forced him to wear handcuffs and leg irons.

Judge Duffy listened patiently, taking notes.

Mohammad told the judge that the warden had taunted him that he would never get out of jail. "One time she came to my cell. I asked her one time as to how long will I be in prison. What I meant was in Nine South, but she understood the word 'prison' and her response was, 'Do you think you are ever going to get out of prison? You are going to be there for life.' She truly said that. She was a judge and jury, and she had already passed sentence on me."

He stopped. "I think I have given you boring details, and I have spoken for some time now."

Judge Duffy put his notepad down. "Mr. Salameh, we're trying to pick a jury today, and the folks have been waiting outside now for about an hour. I will see what we can do about making sure that you are not discriminated against, but I feel for your benefit and your co-defendants' benefits we should get started."

"Thank you very much."

We returned to our seats in the courtroom, Mohammad agreed to attend, and jury selection resumed. I disliked the judge, but I had to give him credit for hearing Mohammad out and convincing him to attend.

The other lawyers weren't happy with the job we were doing managing—or not managing—Mohammad. They felt he was creating a bad image for the rest of the defendants. Over lunch in our conference room, the tension was palpable. Abdellah looked at me from across the large table.

"We didn't present a very optimistic front today."

I tried to ignore the comment.

He continued: "The government's manipulating the situation."

"What do you mean?"

"The prosecutor's manipulating the situation. He's playing games so Mohammad won't come to court. And you appeared nervous and under strain in front of the jurors."

Abdellah's suggestion that the prosecutors were somehow choreographing Mohammad's nonappearance struck me as insane. "I don't think I appeared nervous, and I don't think Childers is manipulating the situation. Stop telling me how to deal with my own client."

"See, there you go again. You won't listen, just like you were rude to me when I suggested Mohammad might want to wear Islamic clothes."

I tried to contain myself. "Hassen, I'm open to suggestions. Mohammad never asked for Islamic clothes." I clenched my teeth. "But I appreciate your suggestions, and I will consider them."

At the beginning of October we entered the final stage of jury selection, when the parties exercise peremptory challenges. These are challenges allotted to both sides that allow the lawyers to remove a prospective juror for any reason except race or gender.[2]

The procedure resembled a parlor game as much as anything else. The judge put twelve people from the qualified pool into the jury box in the order that they were interviewed, and each side then decided which two people to strike from the box, without knowing the other side's choices. New people from the qualified pool, again in the order that they were interviewed, replaced the people struck. The process was repeated a total of five times until each side had used up its ten peremptory challenges. The people remaining in the jury box would be the jury.

The rounds began. The defense lawyers huddled with their clients to decide which two people to strike. Typically, we met in a holding cell that adjoined the courtroom.

Our task involved making a judgment call. Should we keep the person in the jury box or not, based on what we knew of the juror's background, temperament, and the way he or she answered the judge's questions? Some defense lawyers believe specific character traits or occupations indicate whether a juror is pro-prosecution or pro-defense. I was skeptical, but I participated, even though the process often seemed like reading tea leaves.

Should we keep on a man from Westchester? Abouhalima—who looked disconcertingly like former President Lyndon Johnson only with red hair—touched Campriello and reminded him that the county is very rich and that the person in question might not be able to identify with struggling immigrants. We finally decided to keep him on because he was one of the few people who had completed college. Such a person, we believed rightly or wrongly, would be better able to appreciate defense arguments based on reasonable doubt.

Should we keep a Chinese American woman who, when asked by Judge Duffy whether she could be fair, replied, "I seek the truth. Truth speaks for itself." We agreed that she might have problems if the defendants didn't take the stand, and we exercised a strike against her.

We had a lively debate about a former priest, who was now in the building security business. John was suspicious of him. "Every priest I know who left has ended up as a teacher or a social worker, not a cop." We got rid of him.

Campriello remarked that all the prospective jurors seemed to remember Mohammad's name. Mohammad raised his hand. "This is a problem," he said.

The meeting ended, with Abdellah officiating. Speaking Arabic, he invoked Allah, and I felt uncomfortable. Islam still seemed like an impossibly remote and alien religion to me. I had grown up in Scarsdale, New York, my maternal grandmother was Jewish, and most of my friends were Jewish. In high school, I watched news clips of airliners blown up in the desert by Muslim fanatics. About a year later, one of my classmates was a passenger on a hijacked airliner. Fortunately, she was released, but my views of the religion were not positive. I had no Arab friends. Indeed, Mohammad was the first Muslim I had ever had an extended conversation with, and the circumstances of our coming together were hardly conducive to dispelling my negative impressions of the religion.

We went back into the courtroom for the first round of challenges. We removed the two jurors, and the government removed two. Four people from the pool went into the jury box and took their places. We returned to the holding cell to discuss the next rounds. And so it went for several more rounds. The next day, we had our last meeting to agree on our final two peremptory challenges. We all huddled around in the cell to pray, but this time John led us. "May almighty God guide us, protect us, and help us." He had tears in his eyes.

The final jury was composed of eight women and four men. Six jurors were black, six were white, all of them of Christian background, and six of them with at least some college education. The forewoman had previously served on a jury in Queens in a cross-burning case. One of the six alternates had actually been working in the Trade Center during the explosion and had walked down a dark smoky stairway to escape. Yet our jury was unlike other Manhattan juries. There were no Jews.

Looking back, I am struck by two things. First, the jury selection process was not maximized to reveal whether jurors had been negatively influenced by the wealth of pretrial publicity. I believe most jurors, unfamiliar with the courtroom, tended to view the judge as an authority figure and looked to him as an example of good behavior. They wanted to be accepted and approved of by the judge, and so they may have felt that they needed to say they could be fair and impartial, whether or not this was true. This tendency was aggravated by the leading questions the judge posed the jurors. I still believe that the prospective jurors would have been more willing to reveal their true feelings on a self-administered written questionnaire.

The second thing that strikes me is the defendants' determination to participate. These were not people scorning the judicial process. They were determined to be co-equal players. Each had a hand in selecting the judges who would determine their fate. If the defendants blindly hated the United States's institutions, it was peculiar to watch them so eagerly engaging in the judicial process. This would not be the first time in the case that I had the impression that the defendants' attitude toward the United States and its institutions was more complicated than simple hate.

The judge impaneled the jury and gave them some general instructions. The trial would be in session Mondays through Thursdays. He needed Fridays to attend to his other cases, he explained. He told them not to watch television, listen to the radio, or read newspapers during the trial, and he ordered them to come back in the morning for opening statements. I had a late night ahead of me. I gathered my things to leave the courtroom. Abouhalima turned to Mohammad. "Before trial begins, Mohammad, make an application to change your name."

7 Opening Statements

I worked late into the night preparing my opening. I worried. I wrestled with the defense lawyer's classic dilemma in giving opening statements: say too little and lose the jury, say too much and run the risk of failing to deliver. I wasn't making much progress. In fact, I hadn't gotten past my first sentence. "Ladies and Gentlemen of the jury, it is my privilege to represent Mohammad Salameh." No, too stagy. "Ladies and Gentlemen of the jury, we have just heard the prosecutor's opening in which he dwelled on the horrible details of the tragedy. But that's not the issue. Everyone at the defense table agrees that the explosion was a tragedy. The issue is whether my client was involved." Nope, too argumentative. I fidgeted some more. I looked over my shoulder outside. Fog enveloped the city. Through the mist, I could see the vague outlines of the North Tower of the Trade Center, its tall antennae slowly blinking.

At nine-thirty the next morning, I walked past television trucks and newspaper reporters and took the elevator to Courtroom 318 on the third floor—the same courtroom I had found myself in on the first day of the case. The physical setting added to the inherent theatricality of this day. We were in the largest courtroom in the courthouse, a magnificent oak-paneled space about half the size of a football field under a Victorian wood-carved ceiling. Viewed from the spectators' section, the judge's bench sat pedestal-like under a giant seal of the United States. The witness box, festooned with microphones, stood to the right of the bench. Against the right wall sat the jury box. Immediately in front of the judge's bench was the government's table, about twenty feet long, with space for four lawyers, a paralegal, and sundry government agents.

Ten feet behind was the L-shaped defense table, with the long side parallel to the government's table and the short side jutting north along the left wall and parallel to the jury box. I sat farthest to the right on the long side. To my left were Mohammad and John, Ahmed and Ayyad, Abdellah and Abouhalima, and—by themselves on the short side—Campriello and Ajaj. Behind them and against the left wall stood a large enclosed glass box in which two interpreters sat expressionless, simultaneously translating the proceedings into Arabic for the defendants, who listened through earphones.

A wooden gate separated the well of the courtroom from the large gallery section jammed with reporters and sketch artists. (Because we were in federal court, no television cameras were allowed.) Security was tight. Scores of security agents encircled the courtroom, whispering into miniature microphones strapped to their right wrists.

Judge Duffy walked into the courtroom in his usual fashion, telling people to "sit down, sit down" as soon as he got through the door and well before he actually reached the bench, pretending to disdain the rituals of respect normal in any judicial proceeding. He was wearing a bulletproof vest under his robes, which gave his large frame a misshapen appearance. Mumbling into the microphone, he gave the jury

Courtroom 318, where several large terrorism trials, beginning with the World Trade Center bombing trial, were held in New York. After the September 11, 2001, terrorist attacks, the Department of Justice decided to prosecute future terrorism cases in Virginia rather than in New York. Today, the courtroom resembles a closed theater, empty of actors and audience after nearly a decade's run. © Faye Ellman. Reprinted with permission.

a few introductory remarks. "We'll now hear the government's opening statement by Gilmore Childers."

Childers walked up to the lectern. Gaunt and solemn, he looked like he was going to deliver a eulogy. He cleared his voice and began. "It was lunchtime," the prosecutor told the hushed courtroom, and he went on to describe how visitors crowded the elevators in the 110-story towers, secretaries cleaned up their desks, and maintenance workers underground sat for a meal moments before the explosion. "All of these people were unaware that one minute later, at 12:18, their lives would change forever. For February 26, 1993, would become a day that would mark for all time the single most destructive act of terrorism ever committed here in the United States. From that point forward, Americans knew that 'this can happen to me, here in the United States.'"

The events of September 11 eclipse the 1993 World Trade Center bombing, but Childers's statement echoed the popular mood of the day. The scary element may not have been the event itself. It was the sense of vulnerability ushered in by the arrival of international terrorism. On trial were not simply the defendants' deeds but the threat of terrorism.

I listened closely. I had picked up bits and pieces of the government's case by reading newspaper articles, but I didn't know how they all fit together. Here was the big picture presented for the first time. As I listened, I wondered whether Childers would say anything that would be inconsistent with my plan to argue that Mohammad was duped.

First, Childers made a concession. There were no eyewitnesses to the bombing. "Now, as the government presents its evidence, you are not going to have anyone here take that witness stand and tell you they actually saw one of these four men, or for that matter anyone else, actually drive a van into the World Trade Center parking lot moments before it exploded."

However, a web of circumstantial evidence would demonstrate a carefully executed plot, Childers asserted. In the spring of 1992, Ahmad Ajaj departed from his home in Houston, Texas, and traveled to the Middle East to attend a terrorist training camp, known as Camp Khaldan, on the Afghanistan–Pakistan border. There he learned how to construct homemade bombs. During his time in Pakistan, Ajaj met Ramzi Yousef. Together the two plotted to use their newly acquired skills to bomb targets in the United States.

In the fall of 1992, after devising a terrorist plan, Ajaj and Yousef traveled to New York under assumed names. Ajaj carried with him a "terrorist kit" that he and Yousef had assembled in Pakistan. The kit included, among other things, handwritten notes Ajaj had taken while attending explosives courses, manuals containing formulae and instructions for manufacturing bombs, materials describing how to carry out a successful terrorist operation, videotapes advocating terrorist action against the United States, and fraudulent identification documents.

On September 1, 1992, Ajaj and Yousef, using false names and passports, arrived at John F. Kennedy International Airport in New York. At customs, INS inspectors discovered that Ajaj's passport had been altered, and consequently they searched his belongings. When the inspectors found the "terrorist kit," Ajaj became argumentative. The INS seized the kit and placed him under arrest. Ajaj was later indicted in the U.S. District Court for the Eastern District of New York for passport fraud. He pled guilty and was sentenced to six months' imprisonment.

Yousef was more successful. He proceeded unmolested to the secondary inspection area, where he presented an Iraqi passport and claimed political asylum. Yousef was arrested for entering the United States without a visa. Eventually he was released on his own recognizance.

Once in New York, Yousef assembled a team of trusted criminal associates, including Mohammad Salameh, Nidal Ayyad, Mahmud Abouhalima, and Abdul Yasin. Together, the conspirators implemented the bombing plot that Ajaj and Yousef had hatched overseas. Ayyad and Salameh opened a joint bank account into which they deposited funds to finance the bombing plot. Some of that money was later used by Salameh to rent a storage shed in Jersey City, New Jersey, where the conspirators stored chemicals for making explosives. Yousef also drew on the account to pay for materials described in Ajaj's manuals as ingredients for bomb making.

According to Childers, the conspirators targeted the World Trade Center. Ayyad used his position as an engineer at AlliedSignal, a large New Jersey chemical company, to order the necessary chemical ingredients to make bombs and to order hydrogen tanks from ALG Welding Company that would enhance the bomb's destructive force. Abouhalima obtained "smokeless powder," which the conspirators used to make explosives. Smokeless gunpowder and all the other chemicals procured by the conspirators for the bomb were stored in the shed rented by Salameh.

Abouhalima helped Salameh and Yousef find and rent the ground floor of a house at 40 Pamrapo Avenue in Jersey City. The apartment fit the specifications in Ajaj's manuals for an ideal base of operations. In the 40 Pamrapo apartment, Abouhalima, Salameh, Yousef, and Yasin mixed the chemicals for the World Trade Center bomb, following Ajaj's formulae. Abouhalima also obtained a telephone calling card, which the conspirators used to contact each other and to call various chemical companies for bomb ingredients.

On February 23, 1993, Salameh rented a yellow van at DIB Leasing, a Ryder dealership in Jersey City.

At this point in his opening statement, Childers promised to demolish Mohammad's alibi. "Later that very same night, the night before the Trade Center was bombed, Mohammad Salameh started to build his defense." According to the prosecutor, Salameh falsely reported that van stolen, claiming that he was inside a Shop-Rite supermarket and when he came out his van had been taken from the parking lot. He would make a complaint and follow it up in the next couple of days with the police in Jersey City.

In fact, the other conspirators loaded their homemade bomb into that van. On February 26, 1993, the conspirators drove the bomb-laden van into an underground parking lot on the B-2 level of the World Trade Center complex and, using a timer, set the bomb to detonate. At 12:18

P.M., the bomb exploded, killing six people, injuring more than a thousand others, and causing hundreds of millions of dollars in damage.

After the explosion, according to Childers, Ayyad took credit for the bombing on behalf of the conspirators by, among other things, writing an anonymous letter to the *New York Times* explaining that the attack had been undertaken in retaliation for U.S. support of Israel. The letter threatened future terrorist missions. Meanwhile, Yousef, Abouhalima, and Yasin fled the country. Abouhalima was apprehended in Egypt prior to the trial and turned over to federal agents by Egyptian authorities, but Yousef and Yasin remained fugitives. Salameh arranged to flee as well, but he was arrested the day before he planned to depart when he made the foolish mistake of going back to the Ryder truck rental office to get his rental deposit back. On March 1, 1993, Ajaj completed his term of imprisonment on the passport fraud conviction and was released. Approximately one week later, on March 9, Ajaj was taken into government custody on an INS detainer.

"That, in a nutshell, is what the evidence will show," Childers concluded and sat down.

Judge Duffy declared a recess. The defense lawyers immediately moved for a mistrial on the grounds that the government's opening statement was a deliberate attempt to inflame the emotions of the jury. Speaking for the other lawyers, Campriello argued:

> I think there was a deliberate attempt to set up a posture of Us versus Them in the government's opening statement. . . . The government told the jury that this was the first step in a war of terrorism on the United States . . . that the defendants put America on notice. It seems to me that that goes beyond, by a long shot, the allegations in the indictment . . . and that it was only done in an effort to set the stage of, "We the Americans," namely, the government and the jury, against these foreign alien defendants, and therefore I ask for a mistrial.

The judge denied the motion.

The recess ended. "Now, we'll hear from counsel for Mr. Salameh,"

Judge Duffy said. I stood up, pushed my chair back awkwardly, and walked up to the lectern.

"My name is Rob Precht. This is my partner, John Byrnes, and we are here on behalf of Mohammad Salameh. Ladies and gentlemen, the evidence will show that Mohammad Salameh's conduct was not that of a person who was plotting to blow up the World Trade Center. The evidence will show that in the crucial days before, during, and after the explosion, Mohammad Salameh acted as if he had an innocent state of mind, and that's precisely what the evidence is going to show."

I did not attempt to challenge the physical evidence, and I tacitly accepted the government's proof that Mohammad had rented the storage locker, the house, and the van that carried the bomb. But I maintained that he truthfully reported the van stolen hours before the explosion. And what the government would present as proof of Mohammad's part in renting the van that carried the bomb, I asserted, was actually proof of his clear conscience and innocence, because no one so unconcerned about disguising his activities or inviting police attention could be guilty. I urged the jury to pay special attention to a tape recording made by an undercover FBI agent who questioned Mohammad when he returned for the refund to "determine whether he is hiding something."

I finished and walked back to my chair. As I pulled it out, Mohammad rose, stretched his arms out, hugged me and kissed me on my left cheek. I was startled, but not displeased by the gesture. The body language between defense lawyer and client can create a powerful reinforcing message for the jury, both negative and positive. If the defense lawyer seems standoffish and doesn't touch his client, it can create the impression that the lawyer doesn't personally believe in his client's innocence. If the lawyer touches his client and communicates through body language that he likes him—and vice versa—the gestures can help to humanize the defendant. I hoped only that the jury would not think that I scripted the hug.

Atiq Ahmed, representing Nidal Ayyad, went next. Standing nearly motionless in front of the jury, Ahmed began by explaining the derivation of his own name, which means "ancient," and then proceeded to use most of his time complaining about the FBI's rough treatment of Ayyad's family when they arrested the chemical engineer at his home early in the morning. He tried to convey a sense of outrage in his tone of voice but failed, sounding instead vaguely chipper.

Abdellah, attorney for Mahmud Abouhalima, bounded to the well of the courtroom, chanting a line of Islamic scripture. "I bear witness that there is none worthy of worship other than Allah, and Mohammed is the apostle and prophet of Allah." Where Ahmed was stiff and formal, Hansen was fiery and impassioned, walking around the room as he spoke. He accused Childers of pandering to the jury's patriotic sympathies and claimed that the government's case was built on rhetoric.

Standing behind his client, a conspicuous redhead, Abdellah demanded: "Mahmud Abouhalima is asking you for nothing but fairness."

Campriello went last. By common consent of the press, he had the best facts to work with. Reading glasses hanging from a black cord round his neck, he spoke to the jury in the slightly condescending tone of a schoolteacher who wants to be liked by the class. He mocked Childers's assertion that Ajaj was involved in the plot, noting that Ajaj was in jail at the time of the bombing and that his manuals had been in the possession of the government since the day of his arrest.

THE next morning, William Kunstler—who represented the defendants charged in the sheik's conspiracy case—appeared in the courtroom during our morning recess. He had continued his media campaign against the confidential informant Emad Salem and was now dropping hints that there would be dramatic new revelations about Salem. He greeted us in his usual hugging fashion and congratulated us one by one on our opening statements. He gave me a bear hug. "Your opening was magnificent." I doubted his sincerity since he had been quoted by the *Wall Street Journal* only a few days earlier saying that he thought the defense team was not up to trying such a high-profile case. He did not release me and whispered in my ear. "I hope you'll call Salem."

I had other things on my mind. Could Childers prove that Mohammad reported the van stolen "to build his defense?" If he could, then our defense case was lost. Why didn't he tell the jury how he'd disprove the alibi? Did he have something up his sleeve? Was it a gas station attendant we had read something about months earlier? Or was he bluffing?

8 Relevance and Prejudice

In theory, jurors are supposed to separate their decision about a defendant's guilt from their reaction to the heinousness of his conduct. If the evidence is weak, they should be just as willing to acquit a terrorist as a shoplifter. As scholar Samuel Gross notes, however, no one believes this actually happens. Even in civil trials, where the jury is asked to decide a case by a preponderance of the evidence, studies suggest that juries are more likely to find defendants liable, on identical evidence, as the harm to the plaintiff increases. In criminal trials, the problem is worse, because the government must prove its case beyond a reasonable doubt. In a close criminal case, jurors are supposed to release a defendant even if they believe he is probably guilty. This is a distasteful task under any circumstances, but it becomes increasingly unpalatable—and unlikely—as the severity increases from nonviolent crime, to violent crime, to homicide, to terrorist acts of mass murder.[1]

Prosecutors can limit the impact of heinousness by avoiding appealing to the jury's emotions and instead keeping the members focused strictly on the evidence of the defendants' actions.

During the first month of testimony, prosecutors never mentioned the defendants. Instead, they called witness after witness to document the human suffering and physical destruction caused by the explosion. For days, anguished survivors relived their brushes with death when the bomb detonated in the garage of the Trade Center complex at exactly 12:18 in the early afternoon of February 26. The testimony was gripping. It is all the more heart wrenching today in that the witnesses' words seem eerily to foreshadow the tragedy of eight years later.

A hurricane of hot air hurled stockbroker Timothy Lang a hundred feet, dropping him near the rim of the crater caused by the bomb. He crawled in the darkness and came to the edge of huge pit. "I looked inside the pit, and it looked very, very deep, and at the base I saw a yellow glow, but the stuff spewing out of the pit was hot and very smoky. I could almost see the particles and taste them. I sensed a great danger there, and moved away from the pit."

Floyd Edwards, a worker in the mechanical shop in an underground level of the Trade Center, wandered the black underworld with a co-worker in search of an exit. They were down on their knees clawing through the rubble with their bare hands. "I remember looking at Jerry and I said, 'I got a bad feeling about this,' and he said 'me too.' And I thought, damn, we're going to die here, Jerry, and it's going to be twenty years before they find us. We thought both towers done fell in on top of us." He blacked out and regained consciousness when a rescuer stumbled on him.

The elevator in which Peter Rinaldi and ten others were traveling came to an abrupt halt on the sixty-first floor. They remained calm for fifteen minutes, but then they began to smell smoke. Their eyes began to tear, and they started coughing. Ten minutes later the smoke had thickened and the passengers were now gasping for breath. In desperation, they pried open the elevator doors only to be confronted by two inches of sheetrock. They used keys to claw a small opening and felt air.

When firefighter William Duffy opened another elevator, this one stuck on the forty-fourth floor, a blast of hot air, ash, smoke, and soot washed over him. He found people lying on the floor head to toe and thought they were dead. "They looked like they were coated with charcoal," he said. "It was like a tomb." The people were revived, and they escaped.

Port Authority police officer Michael Podolak, sent to the forty-first floor, recalled drilling a hole in the roof of the elevator and finding a dozen young children, most about five years old, who were at the Trade Center on a school trip to the observation deck. One of the first out, a little girl, "was all curled up and scared. She held onto my neck, real tight."

People who tried to make it down the stairs faced their own hell. One witness reported looking down the smoke-choked stairwell and seeing a large knot of people. They were panicking. A woman was crying. A man had fallen down, and people were clambering over him. "I thought we were all going to die due to smoke inhalation," the witness recalled.

Throughout, the defense lawyers repeatedly objected that the admission of this testimony violated the Federal Rules of Evidence. Rule 401 defines relevant evidence as "evidence having any tendency to make the existence of any fact that is of consequence to the determination of the action more probable."[2] Rule 403 states: "Although relevant, evidence may be excluded if its probative value is substantially outweighed by the danger of unfair prejudice."[3] We argued that victims' testimony was irrelevant because it did not make it more likely that the defendants committed the acts with which they were charged. Moreover, even if the testimony was marginally relevant, the relevance was outweighed by the danger that it would inflame the passions of the jury and distract them from the legal issues. Judge Duffy denied all our objections and permitted the government to parade the emotional accounts.

One who survived. About a thousand people were injured when the blast ripped through the World Trade Center garage. © 1994 Richard Lee/Newsday, Inc. Reprinted with permission.

Investigators probe the blast crater under the World Trade Center. © 1994 Daniel Sheehan/Newsday, Inc. Reprinted with permission.

While defense counsel was unanimous in our objection to the victims' testimony, we were less successful coordinating our cross-examination of witnesses because we were pursuing different defense strategies. Atiq Ahmed, the lawyer for chemist Ayyad, and Hassen Abdellah, the lawyer for taxi driver Abouhalima, argued in effect that the trial was a conspiracy to frame their clients. They even refused to concede that a bomb had caused the World Trade Center explosion. They generally challenged every government witness. My strategy was quite the opposite. My plan was to concede as much evidence as I could but argue that Salameh was an unwitting dupe of the mastermind Yousef. I would cross-examine witnesses only if they gave testimony that undercut my dupe defense. Meanwhile, Austin Campriello, the lawyer for the fourth defendant Ajaj, argued that his client was in jail at the time of the bombing and was not a participant. He challenged little of the evidence, cross-examining witnesses only when they suggested that his client did something suspicious.

These different cross-examination styles made for strange spectacles. Two examples illustrate. A Secret Service agent testified that he had glimpsed a yellow van parked in the Trade Center garage moments before he was knocked unconscious by a massive blast. This description matched that of the yellow Ryder van rented by Mohammad and mentioned in Childers's opening. However, a report indicated that the agent had failed to mention the yellow van to investigators who interviewed him a day after the explosion and that he first told prosecutors about it only two nights before he testified.

Even though his testimony about the yellow van didn't really hurt my case, I decided to bring out his earlier failure to mention it in hope of suggesting that the witness was conforming his testimony to fit the prosecution's theory. I ended the cross-examination as soon as he admitted the omission, my instincts telling me to leave well enough alone.

Abdellah leapt to the podium and confronted the witness angrily. He demanded to know how the witness could have omitted this critical sighting when he talked to the investigators. I thought this was a very unwise question, because the witness might come up with a reasonable excuse.

The agent claimed he had been suffering from "shock syndrome" and "post-concussive syndrome." His use of technical terms to explain why he hadn't reported the van earlier made him appear defensive.

Abdellah had scored a small point. Now he should really sit down, I thought. But Abdellah was unsatisfied with the agent's answer and retorted, "Did you have amnesia?" His tone was badgering, and I felt he was risking alienating the jury and creating sympathy for the agent.

John blew his cheeks out. He held his head down, almost touching the table.

Leslie Robertson, a structural engineer who had worked on the Trade Center since it was built more than twenty years earlier and who was called in to assess the damage to the building, testified about the design elements of the building. Childers asked what physical forces the Trade Center was constructed to withstand. Robertson testified prophetically: "It was designed for a sabotage operation, that is the towers were designed for the circumstance where through some unknown circumstance that part of the building would be destroyed, and it was designed to stand in the face of a reasonable sabotage effort. The towers were designed for the impact by a 707 aircraft. That was the largest jet aircraft in the air at the time fully fuel laden out of JFK striking the building at any location." Robertson concluded that the explosion could not have been caused by any equipment malfunction.

It was apparent to everyone in the courtroom that a bomb had caused the explosion. Atiq Ahmed chose to contest the fact. He elicited from Robertson that a fire had occurred when the building was being constructed and tried to suggest that the fire caused the damage observed by the engineer, not a bomb. Judge Duffy shook his head faintly. And so it went for the next month. I hardly cross-examined at all, on the theory that there was little disputing the evidence that a bomb exploded and that it had caused havoc. But Ahmed and Abdellah challenged much of that evidence.

We tried to resolve our differences. In the early weeks of the trial, the defense lawyers ate lunch together frequently, and we tried to figure out ways to coordinate our cross-examinations. We made little headway, and the meetings became less frequent as it became increasingly apparent that our separate defense styles were conflicting and irreconcilable. Abdellah and Ahmed had warned of this very possibility when they moved for severances before trial on behalf of their clients, but Judge Duffy denied the motions. There is a strong preference in the federal system for joint trials of defendants charged in the same conspiracy, and it is extremely difficult for a defendant to win a severance.[4]

Relations among co-counsel worsened. One day, over lunch in the courtroom cafeteria, John made a determined effort to engage Abdellah in small talk. John asked Abdellah about his family and about his school days. Abdellah smiled and described being on the Bucknell football team. The conversation chugged along amicably. There was a pause. John seemed to be looking for something to say next. He looked at Abdellah earnestly. "So, when did you convert to Islam?"

Abdellah stopped smiling. "What do you mean 'convert'? I've always been a Muslim, and my father was a Muslim." He grabbed his tray and walked away.

Campriello whispered to me, "Byrnes can't do anything right around Abdellah. If John said good morning, that would be the one day of the Islamic calendar when it would be offensive to say good morning."

During breaks in the testimony, to relieve the tension, John, Campriello, and I would chat with Childers and the other prosecutors. We swapped jokes, and even poked fun at our co-counsel. I had written Abdellah and Ahmed off as amateurs, unworthy of practicing in our courthouse. They sat at the table and didn't join in the banter.

We joked to help us cope with the stress. But looking back, I now realize we were also advertising to the world, to co-counsel, even to the defendants, that we—the white lawyers—were members of a courthouse elite. We could detach ourselves from the central drama during breaks and chat with our opponents, as if we were all engaged in a tennis match at Westchester Country Club. Mohammad and the other defendants sat quietly in their seats, reading transcripts or writing notes to themselves. What did they think as we schmoozed with prosecutors who were trying to send them away for the rest of their lives?

Six people perished in the explosion. William Macko, 47, Stephen Knapp, 48, and Robert Kirkpatrick, 61, were military veterans. They worked in the Trade Center maintenance department, ensuring that basic services like heat and water were supplied to the 200,000 tenants of the complex. Monica Smith, 35, was a bookkeeper for the department. She was due to go on maternity leave in a few weeks. The four were crushed and killed by a collapsing wall as they ate lunch in a basement cafeteria.

Wilfredo Mercado, 37, an immigrant from Peru, was the receiving agent at Windows on the World, the famous restaurant a quarter-mile up in the World Trade Center. Following his early morning rounds, he was taking a nap one floor above the garage where the truck bomb had been placed. The force of the explosion propelled him from the room. He landed headfirst five floors down and was buried under tons of concrete. His body was not recovered until a month later.

John DiGiovanni, 45, was a dental salesman who pulled into the underground parking garage seconds before the blast. The fireball hurled him out of the garage onto the entry ramp, far enough for people on the street to see him. He was taken to the hospital barely breathing and died a short time later.[5]

Over defense objections, the morgue photographs of the people were passed out to the jury. I looked at Mohammad. He was doodling on a piece of paper.

The jurors passed the morgue photographs to each other. They seemed to linger over one in particular, and when it was finally passed to the forewoman, she looked at it, and I thought I saw tears in her eyes. The photograph depicted Monica Smith. Her face appeared bruised. The explosion had seared the pattern lines of her green sweater into her shoulder and back. Outlined under the dress was the gentle swell of her belly.

As the medical examiner's autopsy reports were about to be handed to the jury, Ahmed rose to make an objection. "Your Honor, on the last page of each autopsy report the examiner listed the manner of death. And I would request that be redacted. That is, the language of bomb explosion is something that I would strongly object to, your Honor. It's something that is part of the government's burden of proof. It hasn't been shown yet, and I don't expect that it may be shown. As such this Medical Examiner is reaching—

"Is it your position that there was no bomb; is that correct?"

"I'm saying there was an explosion, but—"

"There was no explosion or there was?"

"There was an explosion, but it is up to the government to show that this was not an accidental explosion, it was not a natural explosion, it was a man-made explosion. And they haven't done it yet."

"Overruled. Show the reports to the jury."

---

9 "How Are You Going to Feel?"

Two nights later, I was riding the subway home. It was around ten o'clock. I was tired, and I was thinking how long it had been since I'd seen my piano teacher. Presently, I became aware of a neatly dressed middle-aged man looking at me quizzically.

He stepped closer to me. "You're the lawyer for the Arabs."

I didn't know his intentions. I nodded.

"How are you going to feel?"

"I beg your pardon?"

"How are you going to feel when you get them off?"

"I don't know that's going to happen."

"They're going to do it again. You know that, don't you? How are you going to feel?"

"Look, sir, it's not for me to judge the defendants, it's the jury's job. I'm just trying to make sure my client gets a fair trial."

"How do you feel about the pregnant lady who got killed? How do you feel tricking people?"

I decided to get off at the next station, before my regular stop, and rose from my seat. The subway pulled into the station. The doors opened. I walked out.

From behind, I heard him shout. "This is just a game for you!"

DEFENSE lawyers have often been reviled for representing unpopular people. When John Adams, later our second president, defended British soldiers at the Boston Massacre in which five Americans were killed and six more wounded, he was branded a traitor and lost half his clients. Clarence Darrow became the object of loathing when he sought to spare the lives of Nathan Leopold and Richard Loeb after the two young men confessed to brutally killing a young boy in an effort to commit the perfect crime. Edward Bennett Williams represented Joseph McCarthy when he faced censure by his fellow senators, provoking many of his fellow lawyers to label him "fascist." When he later represented a number of Hollywood screenwriters who faced contempt of Congress charges for refusing to answer questions about their alleged Communist Party ties, his patriotism was challenged.

To the critics of these lawyers, and to the angry citizen who accosted me in the subway, the defense lawyer's work offends morality. Is there not something downright evil in trying to get a known villain off the hook, especially a terrorist?

The role of defense counsel in defending the guilty has two broad justifications: to promote truth and to protect individual rights.

How can making a guilty man appear innocent ever advance the truth? The answer is clear when you consider the alternative. The defense lawyer who must tailor his defense to what he believes to be the "objective" truth becomes de facto a jury of one rather than an advocate. If I refused to argue that Mohammad was a dupe because I genuinely believed the newspaper accounts pointing to his guilt, I would be pre-judging and effectively convicting him. But experience suggests that human nature tends to pre-judge: to categorize too swiftly and assume too readily, "to reach a conclusion at an early stage and adhere to that conclusion in the face of conflicting considerations later developed." My all too human tendency "to judge too swiftly in terms of the familiar that which is not yet fully known" can only be counteracted if I am honor bound to ferret out and advocate every fact and argument that can be turned to Mohammad's benefit, regardless of whether they accord with my personal belief about his ultimate guilt.[1]

The search for the truth is obviously important, but it is not the only value in our judicial system. Vigorous advocacy on behalf of every defendant, guilty or innocent, also serves to further "society's determination to keep unsoiled and beyond suspicion the procedures by which men are condemned for a violation of its laws."[2] Most of what occurs in the criminal justice system is not witnessed by any court: at the point of a defendant's arrest, at FBI district headquarters, in the U.S. attorney's office, during searches. In every place, the accused is effectively presumed guilty, and the government dictates obedience. Only the threat that what happens in these places will be exposed in court and scrutinized by defense counsel prevents these points of complete government control from degenerating into totalitarian proceedings.[3] Not surprisingly, many of our constitutional protections derive from criminal cases.[4]

One of the most important is the rule against obtaining testimonial evidence from a defendant through torture or other physical coercion.[5] The courts forbid the use of involuntary confessions not only because of the probable unreliability of confessions that are obtained in a manner deemed coercive but also because of the "strongly felt attitude of our society that important human values are sacrificed where an agency of the government, in the course of securing a conviction, wrings a confession out of an accused against his will."[6]

Will the war on terrorism erode this bedrock principle? Is torture always unacceptable? I believe one may be able to distinguish between using torture to extract a confession for trial purposes and using torture to extract information to prevent the deaths of innocent civilians. I don't think the government should ever be able to use at trial evidence obtained from a defendant by torture. However, the government might be justified to use torture to force a terrorist to reveal the location of a ticking bomb. This is not the place to speculate about what procedures and safeguards would need to be followed in such cases. However, I'm sure of one thing. If preventive torture is ever used, a defense lawyer needs to be present.

10 Cross-Examination

Following a month in which they established the magnitude of the tragedy and described the early investigation, prosecutors staged a flashback by turning their attention to the beginning of the conspiracy and how the defendants came together to launch their common plan.

As the government presented evidence about the defendants' activities in the fall of 1992, I struggled to find a happy medium between not cross-examining at all and cross-examining pointlessly. The mounting evidence had a certain inexorable quality about it. The government called witness after witness to testify about some small detail generally innocuous in itself but when taken together with other pieces would reveal a pattern of associations and concerted conduct. Many of the details were prosaic, a few were not.

Cross-examination is the art of putting your words into someone else's mouth. Rather than asking open-ended questions calling for the witness to explain ("What did you do next?"), lawyers are taught that they should make a series of statements calling for the witness to answer either yes or no ("Wasn't it raining that night?"). That way, the lawyer does not risk having a witness launch into a long explanation that may hurt the case.

There are essentially two types of cross-examination. In a hostile cross-examination, the lawyer tries to destroy the credibility of a witness, perhaps by pointing out parts of his in-court testimony that contradict earlier statements he may have made. The second type is friendly cross-examination, in which the lawyer tries to make the witness help counsel by highlighting nuances of the direct testimony that support the defense case. I preferred the second type of cross-examination because confronting a witness could easily backfire and make the defense lawyer look like a bully.

The best cross-examiners have two qualities. They have a good grasp of common sense, able to sense immediately when a witness's testimony does not jibe with normal physical laws and human behavior. Second, they are good listeners, attuned to the nuances of the witness's answers—the unexpressed sensitivity or the buried detail—and are able to plumb those depths with appropriate follow-up questions.

When these talents come together, they can produce something akin to a flash of insight. A witness who appeared one way during direct testimony is suddenly revealed to be something totally different. Sometimes it is a flippant remark or a callous gesture that undoes the likeable portrait he had previously presented. And sometimes a sudden admission can put a different light on the witness's testimony.

In October 1992, Mohammad opened a bank account with the chemical engineer Nidal Ayyad. In November, Mohammad rented a storage locker. A short time later, Ramzi Yousef—an Iraqi citizen and now a fugitive—ordered chemicals, and they were delivered to the storage locker. In early January 1993, Mohammad rented the ground-floor apartment of a house in Jersey City. In the meantime, Ayyad arranged to have three tanks of hydrogen gas delivered to the storage locker. The details were so numerous. To challenge them all would make me look silly. But which ones should I be challenging? Usually, I didn't challenge any of them. I cross-examined only to bring out facts that I thought I could use in summation.

I tried to humanize Mohammad, even if the incident illustrating his decency was trivial. For example, prosecutors called a witness to establish that Mohammad had lived in an apartment at 34 Kensington in Jersey City, the address Mohammad wrote down on the rental agreement for the van. The witness was a police officer who lived in the apartment above Mohammad and happened to be an amateur weight lifter. Childers elicited that the witness saw Mohammad living in the apartment and then sat down. I looked at the witness's prior statements to the FBI and noticed he had said something to investigators then that I wanted to bring out.

"Do you recall last year that you were working out and, perhaps through the exertion of the weights, you let out a groan, and Mr. Salameh came to the door, knocked on the door, and asked if everything was all right?"

"Yes."

"Thank you," and I sat down.

On other occasions, I cross-examined to take some of the sting out of the government's evidence. Bank officials testified that Mohammad had deposited $8,500 into a joint account he opened with Ayyad, withdrew the money eight days later, deposited it into a second account, and later withdrew $3,400 in hundred dollar bills less than three months before the explosion. To counter the suggestion that there was anything unusual about this transaction, I elicited statements that Arab immigrants commonly open accounts with cash and then withdraw it.

On very rare occasions, I managed both to score a point and trip up the prosecutors, although they usually dug their own graves without my help. In one instance, the government called a Muslim man to testify about Ajaj. I remembered a saying my interpreter had mentioned to me, and I decided to question the witness about it. Had he heard of the saying "suspicion is anathema"? (My idea was that if Mohammad had been asked to do things by another person, he would have been wrong under Arabic custom to be suspicious of the other person's motives.) The witness answered yes, and I sat down.

Then Childers made a mess of it. Rather than let the matter rest and leave the jury to wonder what that cryptic saying meant and what my question was all about, he called more attention to it by raising it in his second examination of the witness, called redirect examination. In redirect, the lawyer may question the witness only on statements the witness made on cross-examination.

Childers asked the witness whether he remembered my question about the saying, and he said yes.

Then he violated a cardinal rule of cross-examination. He asked a question calling for an explanation. "What does that saying mean to you?" Childers asked.

The witness answered. "Okay. See, like if you do something wrong and I am assuming you do something wrong—I'm not sure, you know. I am not supposed to interfere with your life, not supposed to go tell this guy or everyone here, you know, that you do something wrong. I just leave it between you and God, because I don't know. I am not supposed to, you know, just assume things and tell people that this was it."

Childers was not happy with the answer. He tried to rephrase it. "So, if you don't know something about someone, you are not supposed to—"

"We are not supposed to assume something unless you are sure, but perfectly sure, that he do something. But if you assume, then you don't build anything on suspicion or assuming, you know."

Childers was still not content to leave the issue; even after the witness gave every indication that he was not going to provide a helpful answer. Childers tried another angle, clearly winging it. "Sir, I don't know much about Islam, but is part of what the importance of that statement or that saying is is that the important relationship is between the person and his Creator?"

At this point I objected, but the court overruled me. I didn't need to worry, though, because the witness provided an answer even less helpful to Childers. "Okay. Let me just give an example. Let's say somebody, he is married and having an affair with another lady. If you are suspicious that he is having an affair, you shouldn't assume this. If you are sure he is doing something wrong, you might go advise him."

Childers gave up.

But more often than not, I was keenly sensitive to my own limitations as a cross-examiner. I reached my nadir during the examination of an important government witness called to establish that the defendants were apparently meeting and secretly planning.

Ashref Moneeb, a serious young man in his mid-twenties, testified that in late 1992 he shared a Jersey City apartment with Mohammad and a person he identified from a photograph as Ramzi Yousef—the fugitive. On several occasions, he added, one of the other co-defendants, Abouhalima, visited, and the three would huddle behind a closed door beyond Moneeb's earshot and carry on conversations. Moneeb's testimony was important to the government because it was the only evidence showing that the defendants met together in the critical months before the explosion.

"Any cross?" Judge Duffy asked.

"Yes, your Honor, I have a few questions."

I walked to the podium and looked at the witness sitting twenty feet in front of me. He stared at me vacantly. I knew from documents that FBI agents had arrested Moneeb in his apartment and brought him to headquarters in Newark for questioning. Would I be able to show that lurking beneath the apparent calm exterior of his direct testimony was someone who was frightened of the FBI and was perhaps testifying under pressure?

"Were you in the apartment when the FBI arrived?" I asked.

"I was studying."

"And what time did the FBI arrive?"

"In the afternoon."

"How many FBI agents came into your apartment?"

"Seven. About seven."

"And did you see whether they were carrying weapons of any sort?"

The prosecutor Henry DePippo leapt to his feet. "Objection."

"Sustained," the court said, and to this day I still don't know why. But I didn't try to reformulate the question. Flustered, I tried to move the action forward.

"Now, am I correct, sir, that the FBI asked you to go with them to their office in Newark?"

"Yes."

I needed time to think of my next question and asked, by way of filler, "And was that the same day that they came to your house and conducted the search?"

"Yes."

"Now, when you were taken to the FBI office, what did the FBI tell you exactly at your house about taking you to their office?"

"Objection," DePippo again barked, and he was right, for the question called for Moneeb to state something he may have heard someone else say outside the courtroom, a form of inadmissible evidence called hearsay.[1]

"Sustained."

I stood there, tongue-tied, trying to rephrase the question. I drew a blank. The pause seemed to grow into an eternity of silence. I imagined everyone in the room thinking: "This lawyer's making an ass of himself, a real amateur."

Feeling my shoulder muscles tightening, I tried to approach the same question from another angle. I wanted to elicit that the FBI showed Moneeb photographs of the defendants and pressured him to identify them as the people who had visited his house. "Now, sir, when you arrived at the FBI office, did the FBI show you some photographs?"

"Yes."

"Before they showed you the photographs, did they tell you that there were a number of—or that the FBI had a number of suspects in the World Trade Center matter?" But before he could answer, I asked, "Let me ask you, when you first got to the FBI office, what did they tell you? What did they say to you?" I had a sinking feeling.

"Objection."

"Yes, sustained."

Stymied, I decided to move on to a different area, my tail between my legs.

I finished the cross with an air of defeat. I sat down.

It was Abdellah's turn. I was not expecting much from him. The previous day, Abdellah had put his foot in his mouth. Prosecutors wanted to show that Abouhalima—who indisputably drove a blue Lincoln town car—had visited his co-defendant Ayyad's house. They called a witness who could only remember seeing "a dark blue or black sedan" parked in front of the house, but not the make. The general description was consistent with Abouhalima's car, but it was weak proof that the vehicle had been there. Abdellah started out his cross-examination this way: "By the way ma'am, when you saw the blue Lincoln, you never associated it with anyone, did you?" The witness said she did not, but Abdellah had already associated it with his client.

Abdellah reached the lectern and leaned over it toward Moneeb. He greeted the young man in Arabic and then started questioning him in English. "Mr. Moneeb, have you ever testified in court before?"

"No."

"Are you a little nervous today?"

"Yes."

"You feel a bit pressured?"

"Yes, a lot."

I marveled at how effortlessly Abdellah had established the theme of pressure. Abdellah moved on to the witness's immigration status and got some unexpected bonuses.

"What is your status? Are you an American citizen?"

"I was supposed to be an American citizen, March, last March."

"And that's around the same time that you spoke to the FBI, am I correct?"

"Yes."

"In fact, when the FBI spoke to you on March 7, your citizenship was supposed to come around that time, am I correct?"

"Yes."

Abdellah had scored another big point.

"When they spoke to you in the apartment for about an hour, were you there alone?"

"Yes."

"And you were afraid, I'm sure."

"Yes."

Then, almost off-handedly, Abdellah managed to elicit what I could not about the FBI's show of force at the time of arrest.

"And one person was talking to you and the other people were searching the apartment, am I correct?"

"They pointed a gun to my face and they handcuffed me."

Abdellah moved the scene to the FBI's office. When he asked Moneeb what the agents told him, he encountered the same objections I did, but he persevered.

"And once you got to the Newark FBI office, how long did you stay there?"

"About three hours."

"And during that three-hour time, were you alone in the room with other FBI agents?"

"Yes."

"Did they talk to you about your status as a non-American citizen at that time?"

"They asked me whether I am a citizen or not, and they took my green card."

Abdellah's cross-examination was flawless. Through deft questioning, he revealed a witness who had been apparently coerced by the government to give incriminating testimony.

On redirect, prosecutor DePippo tried to dispel the impression that the FBI had used Moneeb's immigration status to coerce him. "Did anyone from the FBI in March when they spoke to you pressure you to make things up?"

"No."

"Did you only tell the FBI what you knew back in March?"

"Yes."

"Have you done the same thing here today?"

"Yes."

With that, Abdellah leapt to his feet for re-cross-examination. His questions now rang out like a volley of shots.

"Prior to March 7, you had aspirations of becoming a United States citizen, am I correct?"

"Yes."

"On March 7 the FBI took your green card, am I correct?"

"Yes."

"That put pressure on you, didn't it?"

"I was scared."

"And you still haven't gotten the citizenship to which you aspire, have you?"

"No."

"Do you expect to get it after you finish testifying?"

"I don't know."

"The FBI has your green card, am I correct?"

"Yes."

"And they haven't given it back to you yet, am I correct?"

"Yes."

"When you finish testifying you expect to go back and ask for your green card, right?"

"Yes."

"Because they told you that after you testified in court then you can come back, and they'll tell you whether or not they'll give you your green card, am I correct?"

"They said they will give it to me."

"Thank you, sir."

11 "You Guys Aren't Loyal"

The government's case gathered momentum, tracing the movements of Mohammad and Ramzi Yousef in early January 1993 when, according to prosecutors, they set up a bomb-making factory in the apartment at 40 Pamrapo Avenue in Jersey City. The evidence presented a mystery, however. What is the likelihood that a person planning to commit a terrorist act would advertise himself to the world?

To place Mohammad and Yousef together, prosecutors called a police officer to testify that in early January he had responded to the scene of a car accident not far from Abouhalima's house in New Jersey. The car had apparently gone off the road. The driver of the car, Mohammad, lay sprawled on the ground. His passenger, Ramzi Yousef, was lying across the front seat of the car. They were both taken to the hospital. That was the end of the witness's direct testimony.

I thought this was a good opportunity to suggest that Mohammad was such a bad driver that no one would trust him to drive a bomb-laden van. So on cross-examination I elicited that the road conditions were good and that the accident was Mohammad's fault.

The next witness, a nurse, gave me an unexpected gift. The prosecutor asked her whether Yousef had said anything to her at the hospital. Her answer had the unintended effect of bolstering our theory that Ramzi was a selfish manipulator, someone capable of toying with a gullible person like Mohammad.

"Yes, he did. The only thing the patient was really concerned about, he asked me a minimum of three times what was going to happen to the car, which I found very curious. He didn't ask anything about the driver, where the driver was going to be, the condition of the driver, only where the car was, what was going to happen to the car, where was the car going to be. And I just told him the police officer would have to let him know about that."

Next, the government presented evidence that Mohammad rented the groundfloor unit of a house in Jersey City, where investigators later found evidence of chemical mixing. In an effort to prove that Mohammad didn't just rent the apartment at 40 Pamrapo Avenue but actually lived there, prosecutors called a witness whose testimony proved not to be terribly helpful to the government.

Carl Butler, an African American in his mid-fifties, wispy goatee, looking like a jazz bassist, said that he began living in the upstairs apartment in January 1993. He remembered seeing one person living in the apartment below him, but his description of the individual varied from Mohammad's appearance in one crucial regard. The person Butler remembered had a "sunken face, with marks on it like acne or syphilis marks." Asked by the prosecutor whether he could identify that man if he saw him again, Butler said no.

Among the visitors he saw at the apartment, Butler continued, the only one he specifically recalled was "a large man, well-dressed with the weirdest color red hair I ever saw."

"Would you be able to recognize that man," Childers asked hopefully.

Butler hesitated and shifted slightly in his chair thirty feet from Mr. Abouhalima. The former taxi driver's red hair stood out as conspicuously as a stop sign planted in the middle of the courtroom. "I don't see anyone here with that particular hair color," Butler said.

John Byrnes cross-examined and exploited Butler's reference to the pockmarked man. While the witness had made only one reference to pockmarked features, John repeated it in every one of his questions, building up this phantom character. "When you saw the man with the pockmarked face, he was alone, right?"

"Yes."

"The pockmarked man was the person you saw living in the apartment, right?

"Yes."

"And you saw this man with the pockmarked face bring in the mail, didn't you?"

"Yes."

By the end of John's cross-examination, John's repeated references to the pockmarked man had created a mystery man whose description matched none of the defendants.

Butler's testimony hadn't damaged Abouhalima, especially after his failed identification. There was no reason for Abdellah to cross him. But he did anyway, and he adopted a belligerent tone with the witness.

"The prosecutors told you in advance what questions they would ask you, am I correct?"

Butler narrowed his eyes. "Nobody tells me how to answer questions."

Trying another tack, Abdellah focused on the theme he had developed so brilliantly with Moneeb—the FBI's interrogation techniques. "Didn't you find it strange that the FBI kept coming around asking you funny personal questions?"

Butler leaned forward in his chair. "I don't know what you consider funny. I don't consider anything about this funny."

I was constantly amazed throughout the trial how much a person's personality was revealed after he or she spent only a few minutes on the stand. The pressure of cross-examination, no matter how seemingly composed the witness, uncovered deep character traits. I was also struck by the parade's fleeting quality. Witnesses came and went, briefly revealing themselves, like fireflies on a summer night, their characters brightly displayed for a few moments, and then they vanished into the darkness, their testimony concluded.

A surprise. Since the day of the explosion, investigators had been subjecting thousands of parking stubs from the basement parking garage to fingerprint analysis. After the trial began, they discovered that one of them had the fingerprint of Mohammad on it. The stub was dated February 16, 1993, ten days before the explosion, and indicated that the visit lasted only a few minutes. The government would surely argue that the purpose of the visit was to scout the location before the bombing.

John and I thought the evidence was damaging, and we discussed how to handle it. We considered arguing that the fingerprint, discovered by a New York City police lab technician, was fabricated. We rejected the idea because we concluded that no jury would believe that a forensics lab would present false or misleading testimony, and if we claimed so the jury would tune us out.

On direct examination, the government witness testified about finding the print and matching it to Mohammad's. John cross-examined him. Without claiming a fabrication, John tried to imply in his questions that there was something suspicious about the late discovery of this evidence. In addition, John elicited that there was only one fingerprint on one side of the stub: normally one holds a parking ticket with a finger on one side and the thumb on the other.

Over lunch with the other lawyers, John explained the decision not to argue that the print was a fabrication. "I didn't want to highlight the fingerprint shit."

Abdellah looked agitated. "You guys aren't loyal to Mohammad when you speak that way. A lawyer's got to believe his client when he says that's false evidence."

John's face turned red. "It's not that we're not loyal to Mohammad, it's that no goddamn jury is going to believe that the lab made this stuff up."

Campriello pretended to read transcripts. John left the room.

Abdellah looked at Campriello as if seeking support. "The FBI could fake this thing, am I correct?"

Campriello looked pained. He avoided meeting Abdellah's gaze. I imagined the source of Campriello's discomfort. He didn't agree with Abdellah's theory that the FBI had faked the fingerprint, but he didn't want to say so. He was wracking his brain for a way to deflect Abdellah's question. How would he do it? I felt a bit guilty because I was enjoying Campriello's predicament.

Suddenly, a look of relief spread over Campriello's face. He looked Abdellah in the eyes. "Ramzi Yousef could have faked it," he said a bit sheepishly.

Back in court, prosecutors tracked Mohammad's activities in the days before the explosion. The evidence raised as many questions as it answered.

Patrick Galasso, president of the Jersey City Ryder dealership, testified that on February 23—three days before the explosion—he had leased a yellow van to Mohammad, who was accompanied by a taller man. Mohammad couldn't decide how long he needed the van and ended up renting it for a week. Galasso required Mohammad to leave a $400 security deposit.

The prosecutor never asked Galasso if he could identify the taller man who accompanied Mohammad. That didn't stop Atiq Ahmed, Ayyad's lawyer. With a gesture worthy of Perry Mason, he asked both Mohammad and Ayyad to stand next to their seats.

"You indicated there was a two-inch difference between the two gentlemen who walked into your office. Right?" Ahmed asked.

"Yes, sir."

"Would you say there is a two-inch difference between these gentlemen, or is the difference more like one foot?" pressed Ahmed, referring to Mohammad and Ayyad.

"It's more than two inches, sir," replied Galasso.

"Thank you," said Ahmed, looking meaningfully at the jury.

"Now, the gentleman who was standing next to me," he said, indicating Ayyad, "the one who was about a foot taller than me, have you seen him before?"

Judge Duffy shook his head minutely.

"I think so, sir," said Galasso.

"And where did you see him, sir?" Ahmed asked.

"In my office, sir."

John scribbled a note and passed it to me. "I think he's trying to get his client a life sentence. This borders on malpractice. No, it is malpractice."

"So, would it be your testimony that he was the gentleman that accompanied Mr. Salameh to your office?"

"I think so, sir," Galasso replied politely.

"Thank you." Ahmed bowed to the jury and sat down.

Two days after Mohammad visited Galasso's office—one day before the explosion—witnesses saw Mohammad accept delivery of three hydrogen cylinders at the gates of the storage locker. These tanks were similar to those found in fragments at the Trade Center. But this testimony included an odd detail: the deliveryman testified that Mohammad had asked whether the chemicals were dangerous. To me, this was evidence that Mohammad hadn't known what the chemicals were destined for, showing manipulation on Yousef's part.

Later that same day, according to Childers's opening, Mohammad started to build his defense. Around ten o'clock in the evening he reported the van stolen, claiming that he had gone into a Shop-Rite supermarket and came out to find his van had been taken from the parking lot. Mohammad would make a complaint and follow it up in the next couple of days with the police in Jersey City.

Childers called to the stand the police officer who had responded to Mohammad's report. When the officer arrived at the Shop-Rite nearly fourteen hours before the explosion, Mohammad flagged him down. He told the officer that he had been inside the store but had come out to find the van gone. Mohammad showed the officer a key chain with a tag containing a handwritten license plate number. But when the officer tried to run a computer check on the number, no vehicle appeared to be registered under that number. This testimony fit the government's theory that Mohammad reported the van stolen to furnish an alibi for himself. He gave a false license plate number to thwart the police if they started looking for it.

Nevertheless, the officer's testimony contained several intriguing details. He admitted that Mohammad gave the police the correct Ryder unit number for the van, by which the police easily could have obtained the correct license plate number. Moreover, when the officer assumed that the license plate was from New Jersey, Mohammad corrected him that it was an Alabama registration, which was true. Mohammad willingly jumped into the patrol car and drove with the officer to the police station, where he filled out a report.

All told, the evidence about the van created many doubts. If Mohammad had concocted the stolen van story to provide an alibi for himself, why had he called attention to himself in the first place by renting the vehicle in his own name and then reporting it stolen? If he wanted to throw the police off the scent, why did he inform the police, correctly, that the van bore Alabama license plates and give the police a very good reason to stop it? How many yellow Ryder vans could be cruising the streets of Jersey City at that late hour? Why did he, an illegal immigrant, put himself in the clutches of the police only hours before he was supposed to drive the van to the Trade Center? Were these actions the hallmark of consummate stupidity? Did they show that Mohammad had an innocent state of mind? Or did they show that he was really, really devious?

As the evidence stood, there was still no proof that Mohammad had lied when he reported the van stolen, and without such proof the government's case was far from overwhelming.

12 "A Person like This One"

Even before the trial began, rumors had circulated that a witness could disprove my client's contention that the van used in the explosion had been stolen from him fourteen hours before the bomb detonated. Newspapers reported that the government had found a gas station attendant who said he pumped gas for a yellow Ryder van driven by Mohammad just a few hours before the blast and well after he had reported it stolen. However, Childers had not mentioned the witness in his opening statement, and I hoped that the media reports, like so many others, were false.

We were in for an unpleasant surprise when we got to court on the morning of December 7. Prosecutors handed us an FBI report summarizing an interview with its next witness, a gas station attendant named Willie Moosh. According to the report, agents interviewed Moosh soon after Mohammad's arrest and showed him two sets of six photographs of different young men. In one set, Moosh identified the photograph of Salameh as one of his customers in the early morning hours before the explosion. In a second set, he identified the defendant Abouhalima. The other photographs in each set were of men who had no connection to the case. The FBI report contained another piece of information. Moosh was now on the FBI's payroll. Claiming that they feared for his safety, agents asked him to quit his gas station job and were now paying him $4,500 a month.

The prosecutor called Moosh to the stand, hoping he would discredit Salameh's story. In a case with very few eyewitnesses, the government was counting on Moosh to identify Salameh and Abouhalima in court as the persons he had seen that night. Moosh, a small, bespectacled man, settled into the witness chair and smiled broadly at the judge. He nodded to us in the courtroom. A Spanish interpreter stood beside him. The prosecutor asked preliminary questions to set the stage for the in-court identification. Moosh had worked as an attendant at a Shell station in Jersey City and had been on duty in the early morning hours of February 26, 1993. Between three and four o'clock in the morning, about eight hours before the bomb exploded, a yellow Ryder van followed by a Lincoln sedan pulled into the station. Moosh related how he had pumped gas for the two vehicles. The prosecutor then asked Moosh to describe the occupants of the vehicles. He testified the van's driver wore a closely cropped black beard, a description that generally matched Salameh's appearance in court, and that a man with a "horse face" was in the passenger seat. Moosh said the person driving the Lincoln was husky and had red hair, a description that generally matched Abouhalima's appearance.

Then came the crucial moment. The prosecutor wanted to prove that it was Salameh and Abouhalima whom Moosh had seen that night. Given that the witness had recognized their photographs in the FBI interview, the prosecutor had good reason to be optimistic. He asked Moosh to look around the courtroom and see if he recognized the man who drove the Lincoln. The atmosphere of the courtroom suddenly seemed to change. As Richard Bernstein of the *New York Times* described it, the trial took on the air of a television quiz show when everyone in the audience knows the right answer and waits in suspense for the contestant to respond.[1]

Moosh left the stand and ventured toward the defense table. He peered at the defendants. Then he looked beyond us to the press benches in the back of the courtroom and looked over the reporters covering the trial.

"Look all over," the prosecutor urged.

"Objection!" Abouhalima's counsel screamed.

Moosh spun his head in the direction of the objection and looked at the redheaded defendant. He skimmed the defense table again. He glanced at the jury. He looked at me. Then he turned toward the jury box. He appeared to fixate on it. Resolute now, he strode up to the left side of the box and stopped six feet from the startled jurors.

Moosh stared at Juror No. 6, a man with blond hair sitting in the front row. He took one step toward him. Another juror, sitting right behind him, began to wave his arms frantically. Moosh raised his arm and pointed: "It was a person such as this."

"The record should reflect that he was pointing at Juror No. 6," Judge Duffy said.

Showing remarkable composure, the prosecutor told Moosh to return to the stand and resumed his questioning as if nothing had gone wrong. He asked Moosh to identify the yellow van's driver. Again, Moosh left the stand and repeated his movements of a few minutes ago. He looked at the defendants. He looked at me. He looked out at the spectators. Then, like a heat-seeking missile, he darted toward the jury box.

"It was a person like this one," Moosh said, pointing to a man with a beard.

"Indicating Juror No. 5," Judge Duffy said.

The government asked for a sidebar conference, and the lawyers for both sides gathered around the judge. The defense argued unsuccessfully that the damage Moosh's identification had inflicted on the government's case warranted a mistrial.

"It was devastating," said one of the defense lawyers.

"I don't think it's devastating unless I plan to indict Juror No. 6," Childers replied.

Over defense objections, the judge let the prosecutor tell the jury Moosh identified the pictures of Abouhalima and Salameh in the FBI interview. In addition, he showed Moosh a single photograph of Ramzi Yousef—a fugitive—whom Moosh identified as "horse face."

During the lunch break, the defense lawyers met in our conference room. Abdellah was deeply affected by Moosh's testimony. He wept uncontrollably. "People think I'm crazy, but this happened for a reason. Allah was watching over us all, he made it happen."

John went over to Abdellah and put his arm around his shoulder. "Hassen, would you like to use my office?"

Abdellah nodded and left the room.

John saw him to his office and returned to the conference room. "The guy is fucking crazy. He has no business trying this case."

Mark Gombiner, the appeals lawyer, added acerbically: "Mr. Moosh's misidentification of a juror is hardly St. Paul on the road to Damascus."

John and I discussed whether Moosh's testimony was sufficiently damaging to the government's case that we should leave good enough alone and not cross-examine him, especially since he might change his mind. Although Abdellah urged us not to cross-examine him, we concluded that his testimony about identifying the defendants from photographs should be challenged through cross-examination. If the jury believed the photographic identifications were reliable, they would excuse his courtroom mistakes.

Hence, my goal with the cross-examination was to cast doubt on Moosh's photographic identification. I would try to suggest that he identified Salameh's picture not because he recognized him from the gas station but because he recognized his face in the newspaper after his arrest.

I started my questioning the following morning. My first few questions were intended to show that he had seen Salameh's picture in the *Daily News* before his first meeting with the FBI. Moosh admitted seeing the picture in the *Daily News* and telling his friends that he recognized the face. I hoped to establish that he had the newspaper in the house when the FBI agents showed him the set of six photographs including Mohammad's picture. Did he leave the newspaper around the house, I asked.

"Aha. I might have put it on the table and if my daughter sees it, right away, she folds it up and she sticks it in the incinerator."

"What if your wife finds the newspaper first, she doesn't roll it up and put it in the incinerator?"

"Of course not," Mr. Moosh said, adding apropos of nothing in particular, "but I was not telling my wife the thing about the bomb because she's a big mouth. She's got a big mouth. I remain quiet for a few days because she would start saying, you can't tell that to no one. You can't tell that to no one."

"But Mr. Moosh, you were telling that to your friends, weren't you?"

"That is why you can see that sometimes you trust a friend more than you trust your wife."

"All right, I think we'll move on."

I next turned to the actual photograph of Mohammad in the *Daily News*, hoping to establish how similar it was to the picture the FBI agent showed him.

"And the newspaper photograph showed a man with a beard, didn't it."

But Mr. Moosh ignored my question and stated that he might have made a mistake in identifying the witness the day before in court.

"Well, you see, he wasn't a fat person. He wasn't as fat as this gentleman," he said, apparently pointing to Juror No. 5.

"He wasn't as fat as what gentleman?" I asked.

"He's a gentleman like this one sitting right here," pointing to Mohammad, "the one sitting. Someone like this."

I felt I had walked into an ambush. Mohammad patted me on the back. "No problem."

I did my best to look composed as I considered what strategy to take. Now I needed not only to attack the photographic identification but the new in-court identification as well. Maybe Abdellah had been right all along, we should never have crossed Moosh. As I wracked my brain for ways to get him off the subject, Mr. Moosh kept repeating that Mohammad was the person he saw.

"If he were to stand up, then I could even really tell better," he proposed theatrically.

Mohammad stood up and smiled at Mr. Moosh.

"Could I go to where he is?" Mr. Moosh asked me.

"Sure." What else could I say?

"Yes. It's him, because I remember that he's almost my height. He was just a bit taller than me. Yes. He's a little taller than me. He was this gentleman who came. Yes, because now I can see him closer up and I can concentrate more."

I did not realize at the time that Mr. Moosh had nowhere indicated in his testimony that the driver got out of the van, so how did he know Mohammad's height? I ignored a profitable route for cross-examination.

Pointing to Juror No. 5 again, Mr. Moosh said, "this gentleman looks like the one who came in the morning and that's why I got confused."

Mr. Moosh's repeated assurances that he had seen Mohammad had a canned, rehearsed quality, suggesting someone protesting too much. Was it possible he had gotten grief from friends and family about the misidentification yesterday and had changed his testimony to rescue his reputation and keep his monthly stipend with the FBI?

Did he speak to friends about the case yesterday?

"No," he insisted.

"Now did you talk to your wife yesterday?"

"When I came back, and then I didn't want to watch television or anything, and she said to me, 'What happened?' And I said to her, 'I don't want to talk to anyone.'"

"But she asked you what happened, right?"

"And then she said, I want to know. I want to know. But she and I are angry at each other. You know, when Christmas comes, you know

When Willie Moosh corrected his mistake and identified Mohammad Salameh as the driver of the yellow van, I felt I'd walked into an ambush. © Christine Cornell. Reprinted with permission.

what women want, money, right on top of the man. And I don't even want to see her because that is a mess."

"So your wife was angry with you last night, right?"

"She was like a lioness in a cage."

On that note, Judge Duffy recessed for lunch. After the jury had filed out, Judge Duffy addressed me in a friendly tone: "I am willing to bet that if asked this morning you would have said, I have forty-five minutes of cross-examination."

"I said exactly that to Mr. Childers, your Honor."

"You said exactly that?"

"Yes, your Honor."

"I'm not even going to bother asking you how long you think you will go because you have no idea and nobody else does."

"That's correct your Honor."

"Just remember for everyone's sake, you have to have some terminal facilities. You have to have the ability to end it."

"Yes, your Honor. I understand."

After lunch, I continued the cross-examination. "Mr. Moosh, before we begin again, I want to agree with you on how we will conduct this cross-examination. I am going to try to ask clear and simple questions. And if my questions are not clear and simple, I want you to tell me."

Mr. Moosh nodded.

"Now, if my questions are clear and simple, I want to ask you if you will make your answers clear and simple. Will you agree with me on that?"

"But of course, yes."

Did Mr. Moosh feel pressure to change his testimony and identify Mohammad this morning because he was receiving a very healthy stipend from the FBI each month? Mr. Moosh downplayed the salary and suggested improbably that he had earned more working at the gas station.

It was time to wrap up. I showed Moosh the particular set of six photographs from which he had selected Salameh's picture in March during the FBI interview. The five other photographs were of people who had no connection to the case.

"Now, this was the group of photographs which the FBI agent showed you on that first day he came to your house, isn't it?"

Moosh looked at the photographs. "I don't remember very well, but I think so. Yes, yes, yes."

"And you recognized the person you had seen in the newspaper, didn't you?"

"Yes."

I now came to the main point. I wanted Moosh to admit that he did not recognize anyone else in the group from the newspapers. In this way, I hoped to suggest that Moosh identified Salameh's photograph not because he saw him at the gas station on February 26, 1993, but because Moosh saw Salameh's picture in the newspapers after his arrest.

"Now sir, besides that person, do you recognize any other person in those photographs having appeared in any newspaper or having been on any television program?" I asked.

"I had not seen him on television, but I recognized this person when it was shown to me here," he replied.

I just wanted him to say no, he recognized no one else, so that I could leave the point, such as it was. I rephrased the question: "Besides the person that you recognized and who you say drove the van, do you recognize any other people in that group of photographs?"

Moosh confidently pointed to two of the pictures. "Horse face, who's this one. And this guy, who was in back of the blue car." The groans from the prosecution's table were audible. Moosh had not mentioned until then anything about a person in the back seat of the Lincoln. Moreover, the previous day he had identified the picture of an entirely different man as "horse face"—Ramzi Yousef—who looked nothing like the man in the photo spread. Most important of all, Moosh identified two people *with no connection to the case.*

13 "My Father"

"Hi, this is the Liberation Army. We conducted the explosion at the World Trade Center. You will get our demands in the mail," the tape-recorded voice said in an almost friendly manner. This was the message left by an unidentified caller to the News Tips line of the *Daily News* on February 27, the day after the explosion. The jury listened intently. A few moments earlier, a colleague of Ayyad testified that he had listened to the tape and was sure the voice was Ayyad's.

There was complete silence in the courtroom as the tape was played, except for the sound of a winter wind blowing outside. Mohammad was slumped in his chair, suffering from diarrhea. Ayyad sat upright and gripped the sides of his chair. He looked at me and our eyes locked. Then he looked away. Abouhalima was reading yesterday's trial transcripts. Ajaj and Campriello were reviewing trial exhibits, never looking up. When the tape ended, Mohammad whispered to John, "Arabs talk too much."

"That's for sure," John said.

The government's case moved forward chronologically, focusing on the days following the explosion, the letter claiming responsibility for the explosion, and the events leading up to Mohammad's arrest. After playing the tape, Childers also entered into evidence a letter sent to the *New York Times* listing the demands of the "Liberation Army," including the demand that the United States end its support for Israel. The letter threatened further violence if the demands were not met. Phrases identical to those in the letter were found on the hard drive of Ayyad's computer that the FBI had seized from his office.

Back in the office, I described the morning's incriminating evidence to my colleague Mark Gombiner. Mark observed, "If that group's the Liberation Army, the defendants are F Troop."

The voice identification had driven a stake through Ayyad's heart. His lawyer Ahmed came up to me at the end of two days of fatal testimony and said with amazing understatement, "I think the worst is over."

Meanwhile, according to the undisputed evidence, the alleged mastermind of the plot, Ramzi Yousef, had vanished. A witness who worked at an airline ticketing office testified that Yousef had reserved an air ticket two weeks in advance to leave the country on the day of the explosion, and that's precisely what he did. Mohammad was left holding the bag. Starting on the day of the explosion, he visited the Ryder dealership in an initially unsuccessful attempt to get back his $400 security deposit. The owner of the dealership, Patrick Galasso, refused to give him the security deposit until Mohammad produced a police report about the theft. The police, in turn, told him they couldn't fill out a report without a correct license plate number, so Mohammad had to return to Ryder and obtain it from Galasso. He finally got the police report on March 4.

During the same period, the FBI had traced the bomb vehicle to the Ryder dealership and enlisted Galasso's help to nab Mohammad when he returned to get the deposit. Police report in hand, Mohammad called Galasso to see if he could come in to get the security deposit on Thursday, March 4. Galasso said to come right away. Mohammad arrived, and Galasso introduced him to William Atkinson, an FBI agent posing as a representative of the Ryder loss prevention unit.

Atkinson's task was to get as much information as possible from Mohammad before arresting him. He recorded his conversation with Mohammad, and it was played to the jury when he testified. John, his arm draped over Mohammad's shoulder, read a transcript of the tape with him as it was played to the jury. On the tape, Mohammad is heard speaking rapidly, in heavily accented English, trying his best to answer Atkinson's barrage of questions. Atkinson asks him the circumstances of the theft, and Mohammad repeats what he told the Jersey City police. He had parked the van at a Shop-Rite supermarket in Jersey City on the evening of February 25. He bought some bags of groceries, for which he still had the receipt. Then he walked to the parking lot.

Mohammad explains to Atkinson: "I saw my friend, he told me, 'Oh hi, Mohammad, how are you, eh, ah, you have a car?' I told him 'Yes, I have a van.' I, I pointed like this but I couldn't see the van." Mohammad tells Atkinson that he called the police to report the van missing, but he says that the dealership had given him a key chain listing an incorrect license plate number and that the police couldn't give him a report without the correct number.

At this point, Mohammad turns from Atkinson and addresses Galasso, complaining, "You gave me the first time the wrong number of the license, ah number."

Galasso replies, "All right, yeah, I'm sorry about that."

Mohammad resumes his conversation with Atkinson. The undercover agent interrogates him, but Mohammad doesn't appear suspicious. He answers all the questions without hesitation. Atkinson inquires why he rented the van. Mohammad replies that he wanted to move some furniture and that he was also helping friends move furniture. Atkinson presses Mohammad. What was inside the van when it was stolen? Did you let any of your friends drive the van? Where were you moving from? Who lives there? Where were you moving to? How did you make the move after the van was stolen? Do you own any credit cards? How did you get here today? Where do you live? Where do you work? What is your occupation? What is the name of your last employer? What is the employer's address?

Mohammad fumbles though his wallet looking for the address of his last employer. He comes across a crumpled picture of a middle-aged man with a moustache. "That's my father."

The two haggle over the exact amount of the refund. Atkinson first proposes $175, less than half the security deposit. Mohammad protests. "That's bullshit." John's laughter pierced the courtroom, and one of the jurors smiled.

Atkinson finally proposes $250. Mohammad responds with a counteroffer that is against his interest. He'll settle for $200. The two shake hands, Mohammad says "Thank you very much," and he leaves. Seconds later, scores of agents pounce on him.

During my cross-examination, I focused on a small but what I believed to be crucial part of the conversation. I drew attention to Galasso's apology to Mohammad for having given him the wrong license plate number on the key chain. The prosecution's theory held that Mohammad intentionally gave the police the wrong license plate number to prevent the police from finding the van later that night when, still in possession of it, Mohammad prepared to drive it loaded with the bomb to the Trade Center. But Galasso's apology seemed to suggest that he may have leased the vehicle to Mohammad with the wrong license plate written on the key chain.

In addition to this point, I thought the conversation was helpful because it showed Mohammad's naiveté. Atkinson was transparent in his attempts to get Mohammad to incriminate himself. His intrusive questions would have put most criminals on notice that they were being set up. But Mohammad responded to Atkinson's fifth degree without suspicion. He was guileless, rejecting Atkinson's offer to settle for $250 and walking away with only $200. He was the perfect candidate to be manipulated by someone like Ramzi Yousef.

John and I believed that our cross-examination went well. But we worried that Ahmed or Abdellah would ask Atkinson about a detail of the investigation that might prompt the FBI agent to divulge damaging testimony about Mohammad. I felt we had reason to be fearful. After all, Ahmed and Abdellah had repeatedly proved themselves capable of eliciting damning points on cross-examination that never arose on direct examination. Ahmed prompted Galasso to make an in-court identification of his client, and Abdellah had put words in a witness's mouth that identified a car as the type his client drove. I didn't want them fishing for information with Atkinson.

John stood outside the courtroom before the afternoon session began. Abdellah approached the door, and John intercepted him.

"Hi, Hassen, do you have any cross for this guy?"

"I don't have to tell you that. I begged you not to cross Moosh but you went right ahead and look what happened."

Abdellah opened the door and walked in. John looked hurt. He entered the courtroom and walked over to Campriello, who was already seated. Abdellah stood nearby.

John complained to Campriello in a stage whisper. "Abdellah refuses to tell me if he's going to cross Atkinson."

Abdellah heard him and walked over to the two. John tried again. "Are you going to cross Atkinson?"

"I don't know."

"That's your problem. You don't know what the fuck you're doing."

"I've done more for my client than you have," Abdellah shot back. "What have you done for the case? You're letting the government walk all over your client."

John's face was scarlet, and he looked ready to burst. "At least I don't do stupid, pointless cross-examinations like you guys. I try to think before I speak."

Abdellah stormed off. He didn't cross-examine Atkinson, and neither did Ahmed. But for the rest of the afternoon he wouldn't look at John. During the afternoon break, I passed Abdellah and tried to say something friendly.

He furrowed his brow. "I have nothing against you. But I've lost all respect for John Byrnes."

I couldn't tell if Mohammad noticed the confrontation. He didn't seem to have a care in the world. He was happy just to be in the courtroom around other people, animated, nourished by human contact. He looked at me intently. "You have chapped lips, Mr. Precht. Is it cold outside?"

The day over, I walked back to the office with John. He dragged deeply on a cigarette, looking distracted and weary. I worried about his health. He ate greasy foods. He didn't exercise. The courtroom was stressful.

"John, what do you do to relax after all this craziness each day?"

"I go home and watch Court TV."

14 "You Don't See the Case for What It Is"

My life outside the courtroom was pretty hollow. At the end of the day, I would walk back to my office to review the § 3500 material for the next day's witnesses. Under 18 U.S.C. § 3500, the government must disclose a witness's pretrial statements—signed statements, transcriptions of oral statements, and grand jury testimony—after the witness has testified on direct examination. The government usually provided these statements to the defense at the end of each day's session, before the witness's scheduled testimony the following day.

It is important for the defense lawyer to review these statements carefully because there may be inconsistencies between the pretrial statements and the witness's in-court testimony. The defense lawyer can then try to cast doubt on the witness's in-court testimony by confronting the witness with prior inconsistent statements. Knowing that § 3500 material can aid the defense, the FBI makes a practice of avoiding transcribing or summarizing interviews with potential witnesses so that the statements don't need to be turned over to the defense. As a consequence, most evenings I had very little § 3500 material to review.

When I could, I went to the gym in the evening, then home for a solitary meal of thawed chili and half a bottle of wine. If I was sober enough, I read some and perhaps chatted on the phone with friends. The half hour before bed was the hardest. My personal life was in disarray. I was in the middle of the break up of a sixteen-year relationship. My sister had recently had a baby. She and her husband were occupied with a new life, a life that promised many years of challenges and satisfactions, unlike the trial I had invested so much in that would end soon. I was now approaching forty with nothing to show for it. A passage from a book I was reading, the autobiography of American poet James Merrill, haunted me. The author described his life as a promising young man in Paris in the fifties. He wrote about having dinner with an aging single man, "perfectly nice no doubt, but to me that day an evil cartoon of everything I dreaded turning into."

The case had assumed a symbolic importance in my mind that went beyond trying to ensure a fair hearing for my client. I saw it as a means to my own salvation. It was going to allow me to re-create myself into the lawyer I'd always dreamed of becoming. But I didn't feel transformed yet. I didn't even feel that the process had begun. And time was running out.

I called Mohammad's father in Jordan from time to time, to fill him in on the details of the trial. "Speak simply to him," Mohammad would always tell me, and I tried to. With my interpreter on an extension, I tried to be honest, telling him that the evidence was "very difficult" but reassuring him that Mohammad was healthy. Occasionally, I would also speak to Mohammad's mother. It was hard having a conversation with her, as she would inevitably start talking about the whole history of Mohammad's coming to America. "He didn't want to go to the States. He felt he would be very lonely there. He was crying. But there is a saying in Arabic: 'Why would you eat something bitter? Because you want to avoid something that is more bitter.'"

I tried to redirect her to the trial, but it was no use. "He went to the United States to get a job and make money and help us. He went to make something of himself, to speak English, to study, to have a future. And now they say he did this bombing. This cannot be the work of our Mohammad—he has always been a good boy, a gentle boy, a loving boy, God be praised." The sense of disbelief that both parents conveyed to me, the sense that it was completely impossible for the son they knew to have committed this tragedy, did not seemed feigned. I would hang up feeling more depressed, and I stopped calling.

As the trial moved forward, developments in the "Plot to Blow Up New York" case threatened to overtake our defense. In that case, radical Muslim Sheik Omar Rahman had been charged with leading a "war of urban terrorism" that included blowing up the World Trade Center as well as foiled plots to blow up other New York City landmarks. Fifteen suspects, including the sheik, were charged as defendants in the conspiracy. The four Trade Center defendants were named as unindicted co-conspirators. The case was based on hundreds of hours of secretly recorded conversations between FBI informant Emad Salem and the sheik and his followers. Salem had also recorded conversations between himself and his FBI handlers. William Kunstler, dean of American radical lawyers, defender of the Chicago Seven in 1968 and other unpopular cases, was the lead defense lawyer. He had been arguing for months that Salem had entrapped the defendants. He periodically sent messages to me and the other lawyers that we should call Salem as a witness.

I obtained the tapes and the transcripts of the Salem conversations and asked my law clerk Eric Larsson to review the transcripts for any hint that the informant Salem might have encouraged the defendants in either case to commit the crime. Eric located two potentially useful passages. In one, Salem is heard to complain to one of his FBI handlers that the FBI ignored his warnings about the World Trade Center bombing until it was too late. This evidence was equivocal. Under one scenario it suggested that Salem was deeply involved in planning the bombing. If he was, we might be able to argue that it was Salem who organized the bombing and that an embarrassed FBI was now seeking to put the blame on the defendants to cover up its blunder. Under another scenario, the passage simply indicated that Salem knew that the planning was going forward. If this were the case, he might have incriminating information about our defendants that could blow up in our faces if we called him as a witness. In the other passage Eric found, Salem boasts to one of the sheik's followers that Salem had bought a fuse for a "test bomb." It was unclear, however, whether Salem was referring to the World Trade Center bomb or to the bomb the Kunstler defendants were accused of constructing. Following up, one of our investigators located a surplus store on Canal Street whose owner identified a photo of Salem and said Salem had bought a hundred feet of waterproof fuse.

Even if Salem had bought the fuse, the evidence did not exactly exonerate Mohammad and his co-defendants. I quizzed John. "What
about it John? Should we call Salem?"

"Why, how's he going to help our case?"

"Well, we can put him on the stand and confront him with the tape.
We can remind him that he bought a fuse for a bomb. He can't deny
his own words. Maybe the jury will believe Salem's much more involved in this thing and that there's some cover-up going on."

"Yeah, but you ignore a danger," John replied. "We don't know
what other information this asshole has about our guy. What if he has
some bad shit about Mohammad? The government can ask about this
stuff on cross-examination."

"But John, if Salem had all this dirt on Mohammad, don't you think
Childers would call him on his own case?"

"Not at all. Childers might be holding back because he doesn't
want to expose the witness to cross-examination, he doesn't want us
to fish for stuff that might help Kunstler prepare his case."

"I don't know, John. We may be giving up a golden opportunity."

"Besides, there's another very good reason not to call him," he said,
as if I was missing an obvious point. "It would really, really piss off
the judge."

But Kunstler was about to force our hand. In mid December, he issued a press release stating he had indisputable evidence that Salem
had set up Mohammad, stole the van from him, and drove it himself
into the Trade Center. By fingering Salem as the culprit, Kunstler was
trying to goad us into calling him, presumably so we could draw this
evidence out of him. I felt sure Kunstler was less interested in helping
our defendants as he was in getting a preview of Salem's testimony for
his trial.

That didn't stop the reporters. I started to receive new inquiries
from the press asking about when I would be calling Salem. Mohammad asked me the same question. Then we got a phone call from Kunstler inviting us over to his office to discuss the issue.

"John, I don't think we should go. He's screwing around with our defense." I feared that if we met with Kunstler, we would be opening the door for him to make new demands on us. What was to stop him from coming up with some other wild claim to encourage us to call a witness whose testimony might hurt Mohammad?

John was more strategic. "I disagree. At least we should hear the guy out. Who knows, maybe we'll be able to persuade him that calling Salem would be stupid. And if not, at least we can tell the defendants we spoke to him."

The court recessed on Christmas Eve for two weeks. That afternoon, John and I set off to see William Kunstler. We took a subway to his office, housed in the basement of his Greenwich Village brownstone on Gay Street. The office itself was a warren of books, files, photographs, and haphazardly arranged furniture. The phones were ringing constantly.

Bill, with his shoulder-length gray hair, looked the image of a biblical patriarch. Despite his radical stances on issues and his love of fame, which he was the first to admit, he was charming in person. Whenever he visited a courthouse he would greet and hug everyone, including court officers. I remember when I was a high school student in Scarsdale being shocked and offended by Kunstler's conduct in the Chicago Seven trial. In that case, he represented a number of radicals accused of conspiring to riot at the Democratic National Convention and had tried to heap scorn on the trial by ridiculing the judge to his face. Now, nearly twenty-five years later, I was here to talk to him about my case.

After he hugged John and me, he led us to a corner of the office, sat us down in front of his desk, and offered us pretzels. "They're very good. The thin kind." For the next half hour, we discussed the advisability of calling Salem. We told him we hadn't found anything really useful in the tapes, and we were concerned that Salem would sabotage our case if we called him.

"But what do you have to lose?" Before we could answer, the secretary yelled to him that Willie Horton, one of his notorious clients, was on the phone. Bill took the call. He hung up. "Everyone calls him Willie but his real name is William. Anyway, where were we? Oh yeah, there's no downside to calling Salem. Even if he has some non-sense on your guy, it can't be much worse than what they've already got, and calling him would create an incredible sideshow."

John shook his head. "That's not how we're trying this case, Bill. We're trying to give our guy a fair trial, not to turn it into a circus."

The offended high school student of years ago agreed with John's response, but I had to admit that it raised the obvious question. Why not turn the trial into a circus?

As if reading my mind, Kunstler came back: "If you'll pardon me, you guys are being incredibly naive. The system is terribly corrupt. Just look at the FBI, how they leaked evidence and intimidated that witness Moneeb. How can you talk about giving this guy a fair trial? There's no way he's going to get a fair trial, and you're only going to legitimize the result if you don't push the envelope. Crimes are committed in the name of justice by prosecutors and judges all the time. You should argue that the FBI was behind the bombing and that it was a plot to discredit enemies of U.S. policy in the Middle East."

"We don't see it as a political case, Bill," John continued. "We're playing it straight."

"That's your problem. You don't see the case for what it is. It's a political case. You heard the government's opening statement. The stuff about America not being safe anymore, all those Arab terrorists out to get it. That's what they've turned this case into, not the guilt or innocence of your client. You've got to play hardball."

There was a long pause. John broke the silence. "Well, Bill, we really should be going."

On our way out, Bill grabbed my arm. "Have you ever been to my office before?"

"No, Bill, this is the first time."

"Oh, look, you've got to see this."

He led me into another room and pointed to a framed photograph on the wall: "That's me with the Dalai Lama."

It was around four-thirty in the afternoon on Christmas Eve, and John needed to get to Grand Central to catch the 5:07 to Westchester. We walked in silence to the Astor Street subway station. Kunstler's words weighed heavily on us. Maybe he's right, I thought. If the government's pretrial leaks and the FBI's heavy-handed behavior with potential witnesses had created an atmosphere of unfairness, shouldn't we respond in kind? Shouldn't we do everything possible to avoid a conviction, even if it meant calling a witness who would only create confusion?

On the subway uptown John stared at the floor. I remembered the conversation I had had with Leonard the day after the judge denied my discovery motion in that withering opinion. John had been there. Leonard said it would be a disaster if Judge Duffy threw the office off the case for incompetence. He said he wished the case had never come to the office. To me, Leonard's remarks had been a thinly veiled reminder that if Duffy turned against the office, he could scuttle Legal Aid's next contract with the courts.

The subway began its sharp turn into Grand Central Terminal after 34th Street. John hadn't raised his eyes. I could imagine what he was feeling. I imagined he felt torn between two roles. He felt torn between wanting to support me in pursuing a more confrontational stance and feeling he needed to be loyal to Leonard. Even if it might be desirable to disrupt the trial by calling an unpredictable witness like Salem, he knew Leonard would veto any radical defense out of fear it would jeopardize Legal Aid's contract.

The train slowed, jerked to a halt, and the doors opened. "Good night, Rob, Merry Christmas." He disappeared into the scurrying holiday crowd before I could reply.

15 A Christmas Visit

I spent Christmas Day alone. The next day, I decided to drop in on Mohammad since he had no family or friends who visited him.

I took the elevator to the ninth floor of the jail. I stepped out into the narrow hallway, about twenty feet long, sealed at either end by a large steel door, the left leading to Nine South, housing inmates in solitary confinement, the right leading to Nine North, housing the general population. Nine South housed the World Trade Center defendants and a few of the defendants in the sheik's case, including the sheik himself. I turned left and rapped on the door leading to Nine South. A moment later it opened with the expected clanging sounds. I walked into the small anteroom, the door closing behind me, expecting my way to be barred by yet another massive steel door. But instead, the door was open and I was waved through without having to submit to the customary search. I stepped into a courtyard of sorts, a cruel imitation of a hotel atrium, without trees. Two levels of cells surrounded it. Eyes peered out from small open windows in the cell doors.

For all its brutality, the space seemed suffused with Christmas peacefulness that evening, as if an armistice had been declared. Guards directed me to the glass-enclosed library on the second level.

A guard admitted a beaming Mohammad to the library, and we began to speak, not about the case but about ourselves. Apparently missing his family, he spoke of his childhood.

I asked him what his happiest memory was. It was a small moment of fame, he told me. He found an egg one day and discovered to his amazement that the tiny veins in its shell spelled out "Allah"—God—in Arabic script. He took the egg to a newspaper in Amman that published the story and mentioned his name. He had saved the article in his battered suitcase that was seized by the FBI on the day of his arrest. "I am famous and so are you," he told me.

Without prompting, he described to me the low point in his life. It happened several months after he arrived in America, and I recalled the period from a conversation we had had very early in the case. He had been staying with a friend in the Bronx, but they had an argument. He moved out and bounced around Jersey City without a job. He described standing on a street corner during a downpour, out of money, no place to go, friendless, bereft.

Sheik Omar Rahman suddenly appeared. Rotund, dressed in white, his unseeing eyes half open, he was holding the arm of a young Hispanic guard who led him to a chair a few feet beyond the glass wall of our room. The guard sat in a chair opposite him, their knees touching. Mohammad shouted greetings and told him I was with him. The sheik nodded, and I called out hello.

Mohammad returned to his youthful recollections, but I kept glancing at the sheik, this supposed wrathful religious zealot and leader of the terrorist conspiracy. The guard was trying to teach the sheik English. He stood and took the sheik's hands in his. Holding up the sheik's left arm, the guard said, "Omar, this is left." The sheik nodded. The guard held up his right arm. "This is right." The guard lowered the arm, patted the sheik on the back, and left. The sheik snoozed.

Eventually Mohammad reconciled with the Bronx friend and made plans to marry the friend's sister. He called his father with the good news. His father checked out the sister's family and learned that her mother controlled the family. He called his son in America and urged him not to marry the woman. Mohammad resisted his father but eventually gave in, calling off the marriage.

It was getting late. Mohammad explained that Muslims do not celebrate Christmas because Jesus was a man and only one of many prophets. He suddenly became quiet and searched my eyes. "Mr. Precht, you will never understand me because you are not Muslim."

I was taken aback. I had tried to make him like me. Indeed, I felt I had gone too far in these efforts, avoiding disagreeing with him and acceding to his demands. Now it seemed that these efforts had been for naught. Mohammad did not feel close to me. He had only declared a truce in his heart with me because he believed I was working hard for him. I wondered whether he equated our lack of understanding with being in a state of war.

WHAT turns a person into a terrorist? Are they "evil ones," as some people would have it, and a breed apart? Or are they like the rest of us in more ways than we might want to admit? I spent hundreds of hours in conversation with Mohammad. I spent many hours in conversations with the other defendants. These were four young men just starting out in life, who had come to America to better themselves. I found that they were serious, likeable people of basic decency until—if the government's evidence was correct—they embarked on a plan to terrorize and kill as many innocents as possible. There is the frightening riddle.

Author Haruki Murakami explored the paradox of what turns people into terrorists in *Underground*, a portrait of the people accused of the terrorist gas attack in the Tokyo subway system in 1995.[1] He attended the trials of the defendants and interviewed some of them. He was dismayed that they had started out as completely ordinary people. Some were accomplished professionals. Yet at some point they abandoned reality and sought refuge in a vision of utopia offered by a spiritual leader and committed horrible deeds. The defendants may have regretted killing innocent people, but they believed their basic aims were correct. In their cause they found a purity of purpose they had never experienced in ordinary society. Even if the outcome became monstrous, the memory of the peace they originally found in their religious beliefs remained inside them.

Most people who join cults, Murakami concludes, are not abnormal. "Maybe they think about things a little too seriously. Perhaps there's some pain they're carrying around inside. They're not good at making their feelings known to others and are somewhat troubled.

They can't find a suitable means to express themselves, and bounce back and forth between feelings of pride and inadequacy. That might very well be me. It might be you."[2]

Ten years after the trial I am still haunted by the face of evil I encountered. The defendants were not killing machines. They were not demons. In them, it seems, good and evil did not exist apart, but were mixed and confused.

16 "I'm Fairly Certain He Did It"

On January 13, 1994, at the end of the day's testimony, Judge Duffy's clerk came up to John and me and said the judge wanted to see us in the robing room. John and I entered, and John sat down. Judge Duffy's law clerk entered the room to join us, as was the custom when the lawyers met in the judge's robing room, but this time Judge Duffy shooed him away. I remained standing. The judge told me to pull up a chair. There was something both chummy and conspiratorial in his manner. He looked at me. "How long do you expect your case to take?"

"Not long, your Honor," I said.

The judge then let us in on his secret. He told us that two of the defendants had met privately with the government before trial in unsuccessful bids to work out guilty plea agreements.

To encourage open discussions during plea negotiations, the Federal Rules of Criminal Procedure and the Federal Rules of Evidence provide that statements made in the course of plea negotiations that do not result in a guilty plea are inadmissible at trial against the defendant who participated in the plea agreement.[1] These statements, known as proffers, are not allowed to be used by prosecutors to cross-examine the defendant, but this protection can be waived, as the government often requires defendants to do at the outset of plea negotiations.[2]

The proffers were confidential, but someone had shown them to Judge Duffy: "The other lawyers, those fucking assholes, they can't put their clients on the stand. Abouhalima made a full confession to the Egyptians implicating your client. He and Ayyad made full proffers. They can't testify. I'm surprised they didn't persuade your client to do the same thing."

Judge Duffy was right. If Abouhalima or Ayyad took the stand to try to exonerate themselves, prosecutors could use their proffers to challenge their testimony. They could confront the defendants with their prior statements and ask, isn't it true that you told us such and such during plea discussions? Neither Abdellah nor Ahmed could risk putting their clients on the stand. But why was the judge telling this to us?

Judge Duffy rose from his seat. "I think your client will be convicted."

For a second I thought I misheard him.

"I'm fairly certain he did it."

I was floored. He had already convicted Mohammad! He had personal knowledge of proffer statements that were unknown to John and me, that were never presented in a courtroom, and that were never subject to cross-examination. These statements apparently had convinced Judge Duffy that our client was guilty, even though the trial was far from over.

I was certainly justified at this point to move that Judge Duffy recuse himself on the grounds that his impartiality was open to question.[3] I refrained from doing so because I felt sure the judge would deny the motion and make it harder for me to try the rest of the case. This was a terrible mistake. In his pretrial and in-court rulings, Judge Duffy had sided with the prosecution, denying all of the defense's pretrial motions, blocking our attempts to have a more searching screening of potential jurors, and overruling our objections to the parade of victim testimony. I had nothing to lose by making the motion, and even if Judge Duffy denied it, the issue would have been preserved for appeal. Instead, I simply held the door open for Judge Duffy as he went back to the courtroom. My handling of this episode is my biggest regret.

I returned to the defense table and sat down next to Mohammad. "Uncle Precht," he greeted me. He reached over and straightened my tie. "Please would you mail this?" He handed me a note. It was against prison regulations, but I took the note and nodded. "I am always asking you for something," he said. "I have nobody else. You are my man." The juxtaposition of Mohammad's neediness and Judge Duffy's premature verdict chilled me.

In the aftermath of the September 11 attacks, the Department of Justice issued regulations that allow it to monitor attorney–client conversations to prevent lawyers from either intentionally or unintentionally passing communications from the client to outside associates who may be planning future acts of terrorism. The parties must be made aware of the eavesdropping before monitoring begins.[4] If a lawyer is found to have passed such communications, the lawyer can be charged with providing material support to a foreign terrorist organization. Based on my own experiences, I believe a lawyer can quite innocently pass forbidden communications. The lawyer is the client's spokesperson and the client's only access to the outside world, especially if he is unpopular. Even though he has not been convicted of any crime, the defendant is held in restrictive prison conditions that limit his ability to send letters and make phone calls. The client naturally regards the lawyer as a confidant and will ask the lawyer to do favors, from arranging for a hot lunch during trial, to bringing a favorite magazine to court, to posting a letter. The lawyer wants to be helpful, and it is in the lawyer's interest to keep the client happy.

There is no evidence that the government monitored my conversations with Mohammad, but such monitoring can be expected to be a common feature in future terrorism cases. If we had both known such monitoring was a possibility, it would have severely restricted our candor. I can't imagine that Mohammad would have felt free to discuss his feelings about the case, strategy, or important decisions such as the decision to testify. For my part, I would have felt reluctant to express sympathy or support for my client, lest I be placed under suspicion that I was supporting and aiding a foreign terrorist organization.

Intrusions on the attorney–client privilege also threaten judicial impartiality. Someone in the Department of Justice had disclosed to Judge Duffy admissions made by Ayyad and Abouhalima in plea negotiations. This information apparently influenced Judge Duffy's view of the defendants' guilt. Yet these admissions were never admitted at trial. They were never tested in cross-examination. Could the same thing happen with respect to monitored attorney–client conversations?

The regulations state that information obtained from monitoring is not to be disclosed to the prosecutors prosecuting the case, but they do not prevent the information from being disclosed to the trial judge. A lawyer has enough to worry about making sure that the conversations are not misconstrued as helping to further terrorism. But now the lawyer must also worry about saying something that might be relayed to the judge, which could influence the judge's view of the defendant's guilt. The new regulations not only undermine the candor with which defense counsel performs. They pose a danger to judicial impartiality.

17 "It Was Misleading"

A prosecutor may not knowingly present false testimony. More-over, a prosecutor has a duty to correct testimony that he or she knows to be false.[1]

By the end of January, there was still a gap in the government's case: investigators could not identify the type of explosive used. Fred Whitehurst, the senior chemist in the FBI's renowned forensic labora-tory, was scheduled to be the government's witness on explosives. The importance of the FBI lab cannot be overestimated. It conducts more than a million examinations each year, and its findings are often cru-cial to both federal and state criminal cases.[2]

Before the Trade Center case, my colleagues and I approached the scientific findings of the FBI with an attitude of credulity. We believed that the FBI was above reproach and that it would be a waste of time to get a second opinion even if we could afford to do so. Few of us be-lieved FBI agents would report findings without an adequate scientific basis, let alone give inaccurate or misleading testimony in court. How-ever, the Trade Center case was extraordinary, and my boss Leonard agreed to let me hire British bomb expert John Lloyd.

The day before Whitehurst was to testify, Childers handed defense counsel a letter that Whitehurst had addressed to his superiors. In the letter, Whitehurst accused principal examiner David Williams, the agent who summarized the scientific analysis and prepared the labora-tory's final report, of pressuring the crime laboratory to slant its find-ings to favor the prosecution.

Perhaps understandably, the prosecutor decided not to call White-hurst and instead summoned Steven Burmeister, Whitehurst's junior colleague and the laboratory's only other chemist. As I stood up to walk to the lectern to conduct the cross-examination, Mohammad cheered me on, "Go Precht, go Precht." During cross, Burmeister admitted that it was impossible to identify the contents of the bomb from a tire fragment found at the blast site that they had analyzed. His admission made front-page news.

As unhelpful as that testimony was, Burmeister compounded it by revealing further evidence of Williams's bias. Burmeister related how, immediately after the explosion, investigators summoned Whitehurst and him to the blast scene in New York. Consequently, no qualified chemists remained to perform explosives-residue analysis at the laboratory in Washington where investigators had sent the tire fragment for analysis. Thus, nonspecialists in the chemistry-toxicology unit tested the tire and concluded that urea nitrate was detected on the specimen. This conclusion helped the prosecution because it tended to establish that the World Trade Center bomb contained urea nitrate, a rare substance that matched chemical residues found at locations linked to the defendant. Williams approved the dictation and included it in his official report.

When Whitehurst and Burmeister returned to Washington, they realized that the nonspecialists had misinterpreted instrumental readings, which only showed the presence of urea and nitric acid. Aware that these common substances could have originated from any number of non-incriminating substances such as urine, fertilizer, car exhaust, or antifreeze, the two scientists pleaded with Williams and asked him to amend the report. He refused. They appealed to laboratory managers to overrule Williams. The managers rebuffed the scientists but permitted them to test the tire fragment themselves. Whitehurst and Burmeister informed Williams that the results were consistent with the presence of urea and nitric acid, but they cautioned that materials other than urea nitrate could have produced the same results. Williams continued to resist adopting the full conclusions of the scientists. After receiving the new findings, he grudgingly agreed to amend the earlier report, but he also asked Whitehurst's unit chief to remove the caveat that innocent substances could have produced the same results. The unit chief refused, after which Williams unsuccessfully appealed the decision all the way up to the chief of the entire scientific analysis section. In the end, Williams forwarded a report including the important caveat.

Although David Williams had a clear penchant for slanting evidence, prosecutors called him as their last witness. They had worked closely with Williams and relied on him to summarize all of the forensic evidence against the defendants.

Burmeister had just testified that it was impossible to identify the contents of the bomb. Nevertheless, the prosecutor Henry DePippo asked Williams if he could form any conclusions about the contents of the bomb. Williams replied that he could identify the composition from the distribution of the damage. He claimed that by looking at the destruction, he could narrow the type of bomb to fertilizer-based explosives, including urea nitrate.

On cross-examination, Abdellah asked Williams about the Whitehurst letter and elicited some startling admissions. Why had Williams resisted including the caveat that innocent substances could have caused the lab results?

Including the caveat, Williams replied, would have "hampered the defense." He had a straight face.

"So, . . . you encouraged Mr. Whitehurst . . . to go out of his way to help the defense, is that what your testimony is?"

"That's correct."

Williams went on explicitly to identify urea nitrate as the main charge of the bomb. His identification was by no means a trivial one because evidence linked the defendants to a bomb factory and storage locker containing evidence of urea nitrate, an explosive rarely used in a criminal device. Prosecutors should have been on notice that Williams was testifying falsely because he had a record of bending the truth, and his testimony was flatly inconsistent with that of the government's chemist. Unfortunately for the defendants, it would be another three years before his falsehoods were exposed.

18 Mosque

Mohammad asked me to go to the mosque in Jersey City where he had worshiped to urge the people there to attend the trial. I asked him when I should go. He told me to go to Friday prayer services. After the sermon, the imam would allow me to speak.

My law clerk Eric Larsson and I took the PATH Train from the World Trade Center to Journal Square in Jersey City, only a fifteen-minute ride. We walked the dusky street, craning our necks to find some semblance of a house of worship. What a difference from Manhattan. The sidewalks were crammed with working-class people, hurrying with shopping bags and groceries past cheap storefronts. Not a Starbucks in sight.

After walking back and forth along the block for several minutes, a man with a pockmarked face approached and told us to follow him. We were led through a storefront door and ascended a narrow stairway.

At the top, we spotted hundreds of shoes, and beyond, a large room, completely unadorned. In it, perhaps a hundred men sat cross-legged, listening to Abdellah. I was stung. I thought Mohammad wanted me specially to go to the mosque; I hadn't realized this was some sort of coordinated event with Abdellah. As he spoke, I envied his ease. He was finishing up, saying how the brothers should make no apologies for Islam, should not constantly fall back on the defensive refrain that Islam is a religion of peace. Sometimes war and struggle are appropriate, he said. I mulled over what I might say, pessimistic that I could approach Abdellah's ardor and composure. He finally concluded to shouts of approval.

A prelate of some sort introduced me in Arabic. He mentioned "Mohammad." I stood up and looked out at a sea of faces—mostly those of working-class men, worn and weary. I felt acutely out of place. What right did I have to appear in this mosque and say anything to these people, who led lives so much harder than mine?

Eric said, "But you're Salameh's lawyer."

I spoke in English through an interpreter. I started by confessing that I knew little about Islam, that I had grown up in privileged circumstances, that I was naive before I started this case. I learned how a fair trial can be undermined and urged the men to attend the trial: "I speak to you not as Salameh's lawyer but as an American. I want to see your strong faces in the American courtroom." There was chanting and applause. I was surprised.

I sat down. The service reached its conclusion, the men prostrating themselves in prayer, and a tiny girl behind them doing the same. Afterward, men came up to me to shake my hand and thank me for coming. Still later, a feast was brought in from a local restaurant and laid out on the floor. Barbecued lamb, grape leaves filled with aromatic rice, okra-laced stews, black-crusted mullet stuffed with savory grains. I sat opposite the imam, an unpretentious and friendly man.

I chatted with Abdellah. Feeling I had acquitted myself fairly well in front of the crowd, I no longer felt defensive around Abdellah. In fact, I realized I liked him. He got carried away sometimes with his rhetoric, but he was never hateful or mean. We chatted as the worshipers left. He told me of his plans to go to Washington this weekend to attend an Islamic conference.

"I'm taking my daughter because I want to show her the White House."

He brushed dust off me and said I had improved, becoming more self-confident when I cross-examined and more willing to challenge difficult witnesses.

Looking around and taking in the scene, I also realized that my impression of Islam as a harsh, reactionary religion had moderated. I had entered the case ignorant of the religion and prey to the usual stereotypes—the women covered from head to toe, maniacal zealots, bombs, persecution of nonbelievers. What I had come to find, on the other hand, was a religion that was unpretentious and unconcerned with status. The mosque itself bore witness to the soul of Islam: a plain room, a certain informality and openness to strangers. The imam seemed like an elderly uncle rather than a superior being. The word *jihad*, which I knew meant "holy war," actually implied any struggle—even personal or spiritual—and was not necessarily invested with violent overtones. According to Islamic belief, there is no need for conversion because everyone is born Muslim, although they may not know it.

Islam had its own extremes, of course, but on some level its lack of hierarchy appealed to me. Indeed, my interpreter told me that the word *sheik*, which I had previously assumed was reserved for lofty religious figures, referred to anyone who was knowledgeable in a particular area. Even I could be a sheik, I thought, if the subject were right. I understood the appeal of Islam to poor people: a deep egalitarianism that endows believers with dignity and self-worth, inclusiveness, hospitality.

It is curious, but until this visit I had not realized how unreligious the defendants apparently were. I never once heard any of the defendants speak of a religious experience, a beautiful sight, or a moment of spiritual awakening. Perhaps they were simply on their guard, but I find it unlikely that religiously inspired people would not let that enthusiasm bubble to the surface. The defendants simply didn't seem unusually devout to me.

I got the impression that they were mourning the decline of a great culture. One day, Mohammad started to list all the contributions of Arabic civilization to Western culture, concepts such as zero, place names such as Salem, Massachusetts, and English words such as admiral, coffee, sugar, cotton, rice, calendar, magazine, and orange. He conveyed this sense of sadness that Arabic culture had not been acknowledged, a sense that the people wanted to belong to Western culture but had been turned away.

The attitudes I heard the defendants express about American culture were often contradictory. Mohammad told me one day that the vast majority of Arabs hate the U.S. government.

I asked, "Does that mean it's okay to hurt innocent American civilians?"

"The average American supports the government through taxes. They are responsible for what the government does." Yet when an unflattering article appeared about Mohammad, he told me, "No problem, it's a free country." Was I imagining it or did he seem to admire the concept? When I explained to him that I frequently disagreed with co-counsel, he remarked, "just like Congress." The same was true regarding his views of Israel and Jews. Some days he would say he admired Hitler. Another day, waiting for trial to begin, he observed a group of Hasidic Jews enter the courtroom to observe the trial. He looked over his shoulder and smiled: "Look, my cousins."

The cynic in me said that Mohammad was staging his remarks, that he was being insincere. But a stronger voice in me said his remarks were heartfelt. One of my goals during the trial was to convey this complicated humanity of the accused terrorists to the jury.

It was late afternoon when we left the mosque. Eric remarked that Jersey City was not pretentious enough to have an identity, and he was right. It was drab and down at the heels. The streets were nearly deserted now, and newspapers blew on the sidewalks. We walked toward the Journal Square station to take the PATH train back. We turned a corner, and then the image hit us with the force of an epiphany. Over the rooftops, beyond the river, the World Trade Center rose up in the distance. In the sunset, the Twin Towers looked like two giant bars of gold.

19 "Do Not Cry"

Legal historians say the right against self-incrimination developed in the seventeenth century. Initially, it was a reaction to the practices of royal inquisitors of hauling people before tribunals without telling them the evidence against them and of requiring the accused to explain themselves in the hopes of uncovering incriminating information. This procedure was frequently accompanied by torture. Because of the citizenry's strong revulsion at the abuse of royal prerogatives, English jurisprudence developed a broad rule—some commentators believe too broad—that it was illegal to force anyone to explain himself, whether he was told the evidence against him or not. The rule survives today, even though the original impetus for the rule—requiring a person to appear in court without detailed charges—has ceased.[1]

With the government's case about to end, Mohammad now had to make up his mind whether to testify and expose himself to cross-examination. I remember walking over to the jail with a sense of dread. What should I advise him? The government's evidence tied Mohammad to all of the key locations of the conspiracy. The most devastating piece of evidence was that he had rented the bomb vehicle. Our defense was that he took these actions without knowledge that he had embarked on a criminal enterprise. But I had only two pieces of evidence of his innocent state of mind, both indirect. First, I could argue that no one would be so stupid to rent the vehicle in his own name if he were intending to use it in a bombing. Second, I had the tape recording of Mohammad's conversation with the undercover FBI agent, when Mohammad returned to collect the security deposit. His tone of voice—and the substance of the conversation—was so guileless as to suggest that he was unaware that he had committed a crime. Could I rely on the tape to tell Mohammad's story, or would he need to testify?

I feared that if he testified, he would be subject to a relentless cross-examination. How could he explain all the small actions he took that appeared to advance the conspiracy? Would the jury believe he could be that gullible? If Childers caught him in a small contradiction, would the jury tune him out?

When I arrived at the meeting room in the jail, John was already talking to Mohammad. John was reading Mohammad a summary of the evidence that our law clerk, Eric, had prepared. Mohammad tried to grab it from him, and John good-naturedly slapped his hand.

Mohammad tried to change the subject. John banged the table. John described the seriousness of the decision.

"I know, I know," Mohammad said softly in English.

John paused. "This is very serious. . . . " He reached and touched Mohammad's arm. "This is very serious." John had tears in his eyes.

"I know, do not."

He closed his eyes and massaged his temples.

"Do you understand, Mohammad?"

"I do," he whispered.

He decided not to testify.

The next morning, the government rested. The judge asked me if I had any witnesses to call. My investigator had found no witnesses. John and I again discussed calling Salem, but we thought it was too risky. I told the judge no, we had no witnesses to call. He asked the same of Ahmed and Abdellah, and they declined as well.

Campriello called several witnesses to say that the bomb-making instructions found in the manuals carried by Ajaj into the United States were also available in popular magazines. He hoped the testimony would support his theory that Ajaj had no motive to bring in the manuals to help the other defendants because the formulas were readily obtainable from other sources. The jury listened glassy-eyed for two days to Campriello's evidence.

And then, quite suddenly it seemed, after five months of testimony,

207 witnesses, and 1,003 exhibits, the evidence stage of the trial ended.

20 **Summations**

The time for summations was at hand, but many unsolved mysteries remained. The government had focused a zoom lens on only one part of the story—enough perhaps to illustrate the actions of the defendants but not to reveal the bigger picture. Looking back, I now wonder whether these mysteries presaged the attacks of September 11. For example, how did this eclectic group of young men ever get together in the first place? They hadn't been particularly close before the plot, and they never showed a hint of camaraderie during the trial. Two of them—Mohammad and Ajaj—might be described as somewhat marginalized immigrants, but Ayyad was a naturalized citizen on his way to realizing the American dream, and Abouhalima had made good money as a limousine driver and lived with his wife in suburban New Jersey. In retrospect, the diversity of the defendants' backgrounds suggests to me that they may have been part of a global network. We did not appreciate this fact at the time. Another unanswered question was who bankrolled the bomb? Prosecutors introduced evidence that Mohammad, hardly a wealthy man, deposited $8,500 into a bank account he opened jointly with Ayyad, but they offered no explanation as to where Mohammad got the money. Equally vexing— who was the leader? Prosecutors in our case argued that it was Ramzi Yousef, but prosecutors in the second case charged that the sheik was the driving force. The contradictory theories of the leader's identity now suggest to me that the federal authorities missed the true leader. The leader may have been Osama bin Laden. Finally, what role did Iraq play in the plot? Two of the unapprehended defendants had strong ties to Iraq. Ramzi Yousef, the apparent mastermind, was an Iraqi citizen, but there was no evidence of his present whereabouts. The other fugitive, Abdul Yasin, had apparently found safe haven in Iraq. This was tantalizing evidence of an Iraq connection, but I think it is safe to assume that if the United States had had any credible evidence of Iraqi involvement, it would have retaliated.

Of course, it is easy to slip into hindsight bias, the tendency of people to falsely believe they could have predicted the outcome of an event. Knowing what I know now about Osama bin Laden's methods—the global scope of his network, the use of sleeper cells, the targeting of American landmarks—the unanswered questions of the 1993 trial seem to point to him. At the time, however, these hints were like haphazard footprints in the sand. They told us someone or something was out there, but there was no path to follow.

Finally, some people may speculate whether Leslie Robertson's eerily prophetic testimony about the World Trade Center being designed to withstand the impact of a fully loaded 707 gave bin Laden the idea of using larger aircraft on September 11 to destroy the towers. I don't believe such a theory. Robertson's testimony was brief, and I can't remember anyone talking about it afterward—lawyers or defendants. The notion that bin Laden or others recognized the testimony's significance ignores a simple fact. If the testimony was so significant, one would expect that members of the media would have written about what it might portend in terms of future terrorist attacks on the building, but to my knowledge no one did. The theory, then, that a light bulb went off in bin Laden's mind when he learned of this testimony presupposes that he had a higher level of foresight and attention to detail than anyone else. He may have, but I doubt it. The speculation strikes me as another form of hindsight bias. Probably many people before September 11 imagined a disaster scenario involving a plane crashing into the towers because they were so big.

THE issue of who has the final say in courtroom strategy—client or lawyer—is a murky one. The American Bar Association addresses this topic in the Rules of Professional Conduct it has developed for lawyers. According to rule 1.2(a), a lawyer is required to "abide by a client's decisions concerning the objectives of representation" but need only "consult with the client as to the means by which they are to be pursued." In explaining this test, the comment acknowledges that a "clear distinction between objectives and means sometimes cannot be drawn."[1]

I briefed Mohammad about what I planned to argue in summation. I explained why I thought it would be foolish for me to try to argue that he was completely uninvolved in the plot. There was simply too much evidence tying him to key locations. The jury might be persuaded to distrust some of the pieces—a witness's recollection here, a dubious chemical analysis there—but they would never believe that the government fabricated it all. Instead, I wanted to argue that the government had failed to prove that Mohammad knew the purpose behind the actions that he took at the behest of Ramzi Yousef. Mohammad grimaced when I mentioned Ramzi Yousef. He was apparently uncomfortable with me conceding that he knew Yousef. He preferred me to argue that the physical evidence tying him to the plot was weak. I proposed a compromise. First, I would attack some of the physical evidence to attempt to show that Mohammad, while present at key locations, played a much smaller role than the prosecutors contended. Next I would argue that he was manipulated by Yousef. His eyes brightened. "Your argument, it is like fort. The first defense is evidence. The second defense is Yousef." I thought we were in agreement.

On February 16, 1994, Henry DePippo stood up to give the government's opening summation. Echoing the prosecutor's opening statement and invoking the potent symbols of the trial, DePippo charged that the defendants had launched "a war against the U.S.," causing "death, destruction, chaos, and horror," and that the bombing was intended to "send a terrorist message to America."

Having thus set the stage, DePippo wove the hundreds of strands of evidence into a compelling story. Ramzi Yousef hatched the idea of the bombing plot in Pakistan, but he needed other people to help him with logistics and to bankroll the project, so he recruited Mohammad. Throughout the months of trial, DePippo continued, Mohammad had been placed by witnesses or fingerprint evidence at just about every place linked to the bombing plot. Mohammad rented the Jersey City apartment where the government says the bomb was constructed, he rented the storage locker where chemicals that could be used to make the bomb were delivered, and he rented the Ryder van that carried the explosives.

DePippo spent much of his summation defending Willie Moosh's belated identification of Mohammad as the driver of the van the night before the explosion. DePippo apparently believed Moosh's testimony was critical because it destroyed Mohammad's alibi, which was that the van had been stolen hours before. DePippo tried to explain away the most surprising moment of the trial when Moosh picked out two jurors instead, only to reverse himself the next day. "What about Willie Moosh? He was a memorable figure in this trial. He was not a complex man. Let's put it that way."

DePippo asked the jurors to consider Moosh's later identification of Mohammad and Abouhalima in the context of other evidence, including testimony about closed-door meetings involving the defendants. "There's more," he said. Early in the investigation, Moosh picked out Mohammad's picture from photo spreads shown him by the FBI.

I scribbled rejoinders as DePippo enumerated the evidence against Mohammad. Before long, my heart began to sink. The volume of evidence against Mohammad was truly staggering. Hearing it out loud gave the evidence a cumulative impact that it didn't have when presented in dribs and drabs over the five months of the trial. I stopped writing notes. That evening I reconsidered my summation strategy. Attacking the physical evidence seemed more unpromising than ever, but I felt duty-bound to challenge some of it because I told Moham-mad I would. However, I decided to switch the order of arguments we had agreed upon. First, I would argue that Yousef manipulated Mo-hammad. It was important to give the jury a compelling theory of in-nocence immediately. Then I would attack some of the physical evi-dence to show that Mohammad had played a small role.

The next morning, I prepared my props. I asked the prosecutor to give me the blank bank documents belonging to Ramzi Yousef that Ajaj was carrying in his suitcase when he was arrested. I also asked for the briefcase belonging to Mohammad, seized from his home when they arrested him. I put the suitcase on the edge of the defense table and the blank documents on top.

Campriello came up to me. "What do you plan to argue?"

"I'm going to focus on Ramzi Yousef, not your client."

"If you say Yousef came to the country with Ajaj to blow up the Trade Center, you're implying Ajaj was an accomplice."

"Look Austin, this is the only argument I have to save Mohammad. I won't mention Ajaj's name. You can make any arguments you want."

Campriello shook his head. "Do what you have to do," he said and walked away.

The judge was late arriving. I told him I would be about three hours, and he told me I could recess for lunch when I wished. I walked up to the lectern. John and Mohammad looked at me expectantly. I began at ten-forty.

I got off to a ponderous start. I thanked the jurors for their atten-tion and consumed critical minutes in an overly elaborate introduc-tion to my main point. Then I finally made it to the heart of my argu-ment. "In fact, not only will you not be able to conclude beyond a reasonable doubt that Mohammad was involved in this terrible of-fense, I think you'll conclude he was terribly misled."

I paused, then went on a bit too melodramatically: "He was terribly manipulated by a devious, evil—I'll say it—genius, a person who came to this country with a single mission, and that was to destroy

American targets, and I think you all know who that individual is: Ramzi Yousef." I added vaguely that the jury could infer that Yousef was in Iraq right now.

Yousef came to the country with a plan, I continued, and he needed people to carry out his dirty work. He found Mohammad, but kept him in the dark about the essential details of the plot. How did we know that? There were clues strewn throughout the case that Mohammad did not know that his actions were intended to further the conspiracy.

To make the point that Yousef exploited Mohammad, I drew contrasting portraits of the men. "What do we know about Ramzi Yousef as compared to what we know about Mohammad Salameh?"

I tried to marshal the evidence indicating that Yousef was a wily, well-connected professional. I asked the jury to recall how Ramzi entered the country, flying in on a first-class ticket, sweet-talking his way past Customs and Immigration agents even though he did not have a valid passport. Soon he was living with Mohammad.

The suggestion that Yousef needed Mohammad to bankroll the bomb was absurd, I said. I grabbed the blank bank documents seized from Ajaj but bearing Yousef's fingerprints and waved them at the jury. "Yousef had the means and the opportunity to bring documents into the country that would allow him to get to sources of money, either in this country or abroad." In other words, he didn't need Mohammad for funding.

We also knew from the evidence that Yousef was a trained professional. A witness who took an order from Yousef for chemicals said that he referred to it by its two different scientific names and wanted to confirm that another compound had the right amount of nitrogen. He showed single-minded determination, resuming his calls to chemical companies from his hospital bed after his car accident with Mohammad. And he showed cool calculation. He reserved an air ticket two weeks in advance to spirit himself out of the country on the very day of the explosion.

By contrast, what was Mohammad doing when he rented the van

less than three days before the explosion? He couldn't decide how long he needed the van and ended up renting it for a week.

Having completed my portrait of Yousef, I needed a dramatic transition. "Now the government told you yesterday that Ramzi Yousef came to this country apparently with no financial plans and decided to alight on the life of Mohammad Salameh, where he was going to get his money for this bomb." At this point, I popped open Mohammad's battered suitcase, revealing its motley contents. "This is the J. P. Morgan who was going to bankroll Ramzi Yousef's bombing."

Mohammad's modest possessions stared out sadly at the jury: a few scraps of clothing, family photos, a newspaper article about the egg he had found, and a notice that he had failed his New Jersey driver's test. "I'll tell you, there are no first-class tickets in this briefcase. There are no blank bank documents." I tried to highlight character traits of Mohammad that showed he was different from Yousef. Mohammad displayed compassion, as when he rushed upstairs to see if a neighbor was okay after he heard him groan. He was naive, as when he asked whether hydrogen cylinders delivered to the storage locker were dangerous.

I had been talking twenty minutes. After twenty minutes, most defense lawyers will tell you, a jury's attention begins to flag. I had made a promising start contrasting the two men and setting the stage for arguing that Yousef had manipulated Mohammad.

Then I lost my momentum. I had promised Mohammad I would attack some of the physical evidence, and I proceeded to do that. DePippo said that Mohammad rented the storage locker, but I argued that the manager did not connect the person who filled out the rental application with Mohammad, who visited the locker frequently. DePippo said that Mohammad lived at 40 Pamrapo, but I argued, weakly even to my own ears, that the person who accepted Mohammad's cash deposit never actually saw Mohammad move in. Moreover, the witness who lived upstairs described a completely different person as the tenant—a man with a pockmarked face. And Ashref Moneeb, who lived with Mohammad and Yousef on Virginia Avenue, testified that Mohammad did not leave that apartment until February, well after the time he was supposedly living at 40 Pamrapo. Sure, Mohammad might have been present at 40 Pamrapo from time to time (I couldn't deny his fingerprints), but there was no proof he actually lived there.

I paused, aware that this rebuttal was not sounding as strong as my earlier argument that he was duped. Several jurors had stopped looking at me. I plunged ahead.

DePippo claimed that Mohammad was mixing chemicals at 40 Pamrapo, but I noted that according to Agent Williams, such mixing would have caused noxious fumes, and Mr. Butler—Mohammad's upstairs neighbor at 40 Pamrapo—never testified to smelling or hearing anything unusual. I attacked DePippo for assuming that chemically stained jeans, waist size 30, belonged to Mohammad. "How does the government know that Mr. Salameh wears a size 30 jean?" Besides, Mohammad's skin showed no traces of the yellowing that occurs when someone handles nitroglycerin.

By now, none of the jurors was looking at me. I got the definite sense that I was losing them, barely an hour into my summation. I suggested to the court that it might be a convenient time to break for lunch.

I walked back to my office feeling drained and defeated. I closed my door and sat down, dreading the second half, alternately trying to figure out how to salvage my summation and wishing I were someplace else. For a moment, I wondered: what if I just don't show up for the second half?

I imagined the scene: John searching for me frantically and returning to the defense table to try to calm Mohammad; more agonizing minutes as they waited to see if I would finally show up, amid a growing buzz from the spectator section; the clerk coming up to John and telling him to go to the judge's robing room; John, red-faced, admitting he didn't know where I was; the judge coming out and adjourning the case for the rest of the day, telling the jury not to speculate about why there would be a delay, but everyone knowing why; the newspaper reporters bounding from the courtroom with a juicy story; finally, the newspaper headlines the next morning, sealing my humiliation.

I returned to the courtroom.

The detour I had taken to rebut the evidence piece by piece had not gone well. I decided to shorten this part of the summation and return as quickly as possible to the dupe theme. But there was still one piece of physical evidence to deal with: the parking ticket bearing Mohammad's print and indicating that he had made a brief visit to the World Trade Center garage on February 16—ten days before the bombing. If I ignored it, the prosecutor would clobber me with it in his rebuttal. The problem: I was stumped as to how to neutralize it. I feared losing credibility if I claimed that the authorities had manufactured the print. Tiptoeing, I argued timidly that the discovery of the ticket only after the trial began and by the New York City Police Department—not federal investigators—cast doubt on the ticket's "validity." I didn't elaborate.

Now I could get back to the dupe defense. But before I could plausibly argue that Yousef had manipulated Mohammad, I had to explain why he needed Mohammad in the first place. "Now, the important thing to remember here is Ramzi Yousef's Iraqi connection," I said, as if the jurors would immediately understand. "You know, I don't have to dwell with you on the significance of Iraq in American history. Suffice it to say that had Ramzi Yousef's activities been traced back to Iraq, not only Mr. Ramzi Yousef but Iraq would be in trouble." Hence, Yousef needed someone who would do his dirty work without asking a lot of questions, someone who would put distance between Yousef and his activities, and someone he could discard without having to buy him a ticket out of the country. And how do you manage such a person? "You do that by telling them as little as possible."

Next, I had to defend Mohammad's alibi. What proof did the government have that Mohammad falsely reported the van stolen and actually drove it to the Trade Center? Mr. Moosh. DePippo had relied on Moosh's testimony to disprove Mohammad's story, so I went through the predictable attacks on Moosh's credibility. What other evidence did we have that Mr. Moosh was mistaken? "We have the evidence that Mr. Salameh is one of the world's worst drivers."

I tried to create a mental picture for the jury. "Figure this, ladies and gentleman. You're Ramzi Yousef. You are traveling home one night on January 24th. The roads are absolutely clear. There's no ice. There's no snow. The area is well lit. You are in the passenger seat of this automobile, and this automobile driven by Mohammad Salameh fails to navigate a very simple curve in the road. All of a sudden, they are in an automobile accident. Mr. Salameh is flat on his back on the frozen ground, and Mr. Ramzi Yousef is slumped over in the front of the car on the passenger side. At this moment, a brilliant idea occurs to Ramzi Yousef. Now I know who I want to drive the bomb!"

Several jurors were smiling.

"Now, according to the government's theory, Ramzi Yousef thinks this is such a great idea that he insists on pursuing it even after Mr. Salameh is involved in yet another accident a couple of weeks later. 'You mean you've flunked your road test, Mohammad? No problem. This is really not a very important drive. And you know what? I've had such great experiences with you in the past, I'm going to ride as your passenger to the World Trade Center,' because that's what Mr. Moosh said."

The jurors were laughing now, and a good portion of the spectators as well. I had gotten the jury to laugh at the government's theory.

I felt I had regained some lost momentum. I returned to the theme of Yousef's coldly calculating personality—the testimony of the first aid volunteer who treated Yousef at the scene of the car accident. The only thing Yousef was concerned about, the volunteer said, was what was going to happen to the car. He didn't ask anything about the driver, Mohammad, where he had been taken or what his medical condition was. "That piece of evidence, I submit to you, ladies and gentlemen, is a very telling, a very clear reflection of the mind and psychology of Ramzi Yousef. He uses people. He doesn't give a damn about them. And when he's finished using them, he discards them."

How do we know that Mohammad was without criminal intent when he rented the yellow van? He did nothing to disguise his identity or whereabouts on the rental application.

I asked for a break. Mohammad looked at me impassively. He was silent.

Continuing after the break, I tried to neutralize DePippo's argument that Mohammad had manufactured the story about the stolen van to furnish himself with an alibi. I fell back on common sense. Mohammad's behavior toward the police was natural if he was honestly reporting the van stolen but completely bizarre if he was going to use the van later that night to drive the bomb. He contacted the police to report the van stolen, presented them with a key chain from the Ryder dealership bearing a license number that did not check out on the police computers, then told them correctly that the van had Alabama plates, and agreed to accompany the officers to the station.

"Here he is giving this information to the police, it's not checking out, he's an illegal immigrant, he doesn't know what's going to happen at the police station. And yet, if you believe the government's theory, Mohammad is a man with some very important business that night, putting himself in the clutches of the police, giving them information that doesn't check out, and risking being detained."

"But if you have any doubt in your mind about Mr. Salameh's innocent state of mind," I said with as much earnestness I could muster, "listen to this most extraordinary tape of the conversation that occurs on March 4th."

I tried to build up the recording. "Throughout this trial there has been very little direct evidence about the defendants here. We have had a lot of conflicting testimony. We have fingerprints. We have pieces of metal. We have volumes of books and papers. What we don't have is a clear, rounded, flesh-like portrait of a person, something real, something we can touch, something we can relate to, something we can weigh in our hands and evaluate."

"But here, through the existence of this recording, in marked contrast to the murkiness and dryness of the other trial evidence, we do have a portrait of a real person, a spotlight put on a human being, Mohammad Salameh, and the spotlight occurs because Mohammad is recorded by Agent Atkinson when he returns for the deposit."

I summarized the conversation. Atkinson, posing as a representative of Ryder's loss prevention unit, interrogates Mohammad, asking him scores of questions that have no conceivable relevance to theft prevention. The questions would put any guilty person on notice that he was being set up by law enforcement, but Mohammad answers them all forthrightly and without hesitation.

"Don't just listen to the answers," I said. "Equally importantly, listen to his tone of voice, and ask yourself, is this the tone of voice of someone who has just successfully blown up the Trade Center?" I hoped that the sincerity of his voice, so apparent to me, would impress the jurors as well. "Or is this the tone of a voice of a simple man, unpretentious, sincere, polite, a struggling immigrant who needs the meager money back because he lives on the margin?"

I hoped to drive home the point by directing the jurors to a particular exchange in the recording. "There is, I think, a very (for me at any rate) touching point where he's rifling through his wallet to give Agent Atkinson all the information he wants, and all of a sudden, he comes upon a picture of his father, and he says, in a very sweet, wistful way, because his father is abroad in Jordan, 'Oh, this is a picture of my father.'"

"Listen to the passage, ladies and gentleman. It tells you a lot about this man." I looked momentarily at Mohammad, and I saw tears in his eyes.

I felt it was time to end.

"Listen to that conversation. See how Mr. Atkinson is leading him along in that conversation, how Mr. Atkinson is talking him out of his money. And how, despite all those questions, Mr. Salameh is not suspicious.

"He is not a suspicious man. He is an innocent man.

"Thank you."

Mohammad did not embrace me as he had after my opening statement, but as I gathered my papers I felt at least the second half of my summation had gone better than the first. "Good job," John said, patting me on the back.

I got back home around six in the evening and turned on the television news to see if there were any stories about the summation. I was only mildly surprised that the summation was the lead story on several channels, but I was startled by the tenor of the reports. Several reporters said that I had stunned the courtroom by admitting the existence of a bombing conspiracy and my client's involvement in it. From my standpoint, I had done nothing unusual. I had merely admitted what I had to—that there was a plot and that Mohammad was present—and then had gone on to argue that he had an innocent state of mind.

21   "I Could Not Believe My Ears"

I was feeling buoyant when I got to the courtroom next morning, but none of the other lawyers was there. A marshal directed me to go to the judge's robing room. I knocked and entered. The other lawyers and the judge were listening to Campriello.

"Your Honor, I asked to be permitted to address the court. Basically, my reason is to ask the court to grant Mr. Ajaj a mistrial. In my view, Mr. Precht did more damage to Mr. Ajaj in the first six minutes or so of his summation than Mr. DePippo did in the six hours of his summation."

Campriello's posturing, I thought.

"What I think happened went beyond the antagonistic defenses and really made Mr. Ajaj find himself in a position where he has two prosecutors; one, the government and, one, Mr. Precht."

I knew he needed to make a record for the appeal. But I was annoyed that he described me as another prosecutor.

"I will be frank with the court," Campriello continued. "I did know ahead of time that Mr. Precht intended to put weight on Ramzi Yousef. And I understand that. And I understand the reasons for that. What I did not know ahead of time, other than actually within moments of the beginning of the summation, was that Mr. Precht had bought into what I think is Mr. DePippo's view of the case, namely, that Ramzi Yousef came to this country with a plan already in mind, to blow up the World Trade Center. And, I will note that Mr. Precht showed the jury evidence seized from my client and attributed the evidence to Yousef. That implicates my client. For these reasons I again ask for a mistrial."

"No. No." Judge Duffy replied. "It may have been Mr. Salameh's best chance."

When I returned to the courtroom, the defendants avoided eye contact with me. We sat down to hear Ahmed's summation. For perhaps an hour or so, he studiously avoided talking about the evidence, singing praises to the U.S. Constitution and returning to his opening theme of the dastardly fashion in which the federal authorities treated his client's family. Judge Duffy closed his eyes. Ahmed droned on. I doodled. When would Ahmed start talking about the evidence? I could hear the spectators murmuring in the courtroom.

The time for the midmorning break approached. Ahmed finished his sentence and turned to the judge, "Is this a good time, your Honor?"

There was no response from the judge. He sat immobile, eyes shut. The silence stretched out. Still Judge Duffy didn't stir. Abdellah cleared his throat loudly. Judge Duffy opened his eyes dramatically, with a start. Abdellah's action, and the judge's theatrical response, somehow reminded me of Captain Kangaroo awakening the slumbering Grandfather Clock on the old television program, its gray immobile face suddenly coming to life. Ahmed offered again meekly: "Is this a good time to break, your Honor?"

"Sure. If you want, why not? Ladies and gentlemen, we will take a break."

After the break, Ahmed resumed and quickly got himself into more trouble. He attempted to offer an explanation as to why his client opened a joint bank account with Mohammad and started placing orders for chemicals. There was no evidence in the record, but Ahmed proclaimed: "Mr. Ayyad was going to start a chemical export business."

A short time later, Judge Duffy recessed for lunch. The jury left the courtroom. Ahmed gathered his papers. Judge Duffy shot him a dirty look. "You suggested you would prove certain things, and you didn't. And yet you have summed up as though they are in the record."

Ahmed protested. "Your Honor, I am drawing certain inferences, and that's what I am trying to tell—"

"Yes, but you can't make it up," the judge interrupted. "You've come out with things that have absolutely no basis in the record."

After the lunch recess, Ahmed meandered some more. Time stood still. Finally, he appeared to be concluding. He looked at the jury solemnly. The government has a heavy burden, he told them. "If each and every one of those elements for each count is proven beyond a reasonable doubt and up to a moral certainty, then you reach a very simple decision—"

"Your Honor." Childers shot up from his chair, startling the jurors. "I object to the 'moral certainty' reference."

Judge Duffy shook his head. "That's not the law, Mr. Ahmed. I don't know where that came from."

"Well, it's a high burden anyway, ladies and gentlemen," Ahmed said, and he finished.

In the late afternoon, Abdellah began his summation. Springing into the well of the courtroom like a lion tamer, Abdellah was everything Ahmed was not: lively, forceful, riveting. He accused the government of deception. He bounded to the witness chair, sat in it, and reminded the jurors of Mr. Moosh. For Abdellah, Moosh's misidentification of the jurors was a defining moment. He lashed out at De-Pippo for suggesting that the error was a simple mistake, later corrected. He leaned toward the jury from the witness chair. "He didn't make no mistake. He picked the wrong man 'cause he never saw Mr. Abouhalima. That's why he picked the wrong man. That's the reason he picked the wrong man."

He spoke to the jurors as if he were a preacher in a revival meeting describing a miracle, caught up in his enthusiasm, not worrying if his speech was always grammatical or logical. "See, ladies and gentlemen, people like to—see, we've been told throughout the whole case that what we saw was something different, and at first, I say, well, maybe, you know, people like me, basketball, football, maybe we seeing something different. But as the case progressed I became convinced that my vision is clear, and when Moosh came in here and picked the wrong person, it certified to me that my vision is clear, 'cause there was no clearer proof for me in this case than Mr. Moosh picking two jurors."

Abdellah's summation electrified the courtroom after Ahmed's leaden performance. He attacked the government for wrapping itself in the flag. "Don't let nobody sell you this trip about an acquittal mean you unpatriotic." When he concluded for the day, you could see him almost floating on the good will of the people in the courtroom who admired his passion.

The next morning, Thursday, I learned that Mohammad had written a letter to the judge complaining about my summation. I was surprised. The second half of the summation had gone well. I had even moved Mohammad to tears. I questioned Mohammad about the letter in the few moments we had before Abdellah resumed.

"Nothing personal," he said, "I do not discuss facts."

"Do you want a new lawyer?"

"No, no, you are my lawyer."

The judge had placed the letter under seal and out of the hands of the press. I didn't see it and tried to put it out of my mind.

Abdellah took to the floor again, but I felt he was off. His religious fervor was gone. Now he sounded strident and shrill as he set about challenging the government's physical evidence, piece by piece. He indulged some of his strange pet theories, including that the yellow van Mohammad rented was actually returned to the dealership before the explosion. I thought he dissipated the excitement he had created the day before.

Now, late in the day, Campriello began his summation. He didn't get far. Judge Duffy adjourned for the weekend, telling everyone to come back Tuesday, the day after President's Day. I looked forward to the long weekend. I needed a rest before the ordeal of sweating out the wait for the verdict.

WHAT started out as a pleasant weekend turned into a nightmare.

I enjoyed the unseasonably warm weather, bought half a dozen CDs at Tower Records, and bought a sweater at Barney's. I read a transcript of my summation and felt modestly satisfied with it. Yes, at points I managed to put a new light on the evidence and to humanize Mohammad. Monday was a glorious day. I walked to the Museum of Modern Art to catch an exhibit, grabbed a bus uptown to Fairway where I bought some Parma ham, and walked all the way home in a peaceful mood.

I had just finished a glass of wine when the phone rang. It was Jean King, a reporter from Reuters, calling to tell me she had just concluded a telephone interview with Mohammad. I was alarmed. This was the first time Mohammad had disregarded my instructions and spoken to the press. The news got worse. According to King, Mohammad bitterly attacked me for saying there was a conspiracy to blow up the Trade Center and for maintaining that the mastermind had duped him.

King described Mohammad's comments to her. He told her he had sent a letter to the judge saying that the summation did not represent his views. "I could not believe my ears," he told the reporter. "Mr. Precht did not consult me first and totally changed everything we had agreed on three days earlier."

"Of course I'm angry. I thought I was going to die when Mr. Precht started to say what he said to the jury. I tried to stay calm, but it was a shock. I could not believe my ears. At first, I thought the interpreter was making a mistake.

"I had absolutely no knowledge beforehand what he was going to say. What he told the jury does not represent me. He only represented his own views."

He explained to King why he was telling the world. "My aim is to tell people I did not do anything. I am innocent. Mr. Precht knows in his heart I am innocent. But to prove me innocent, it has to be done the right way, not Precht's way."

King asked for my reaction, and I told her I would have no comment.

By Tuesday morning Mohammad's denunciation had hit all the newspapers. The tabloids were now reporting that Mohammad accused me of betraying him. Legal experts were quoted as saying that there might now be grounds for an appeal because I had denied Mohammad his right to participate in his own defense. A crowd of reporters waited for me at the entrance of the courthouse, and cameras clicked away as I ran through the gauntlet, waving off their questions.

I stood in the hallway trying to collect myself. I saw my interpreter and asked him what the reaction was in the Arabic community. The rumor going around was that I secretly worked for the U.S. government, he told me.

Ahmed saw us and approached. "Ajaj and Abouhalima believe you've been bought off."

John butted in. "Don't worry Rob, no one will blame you. Mohammad's just acting like an asshole."

When I sat down next to Mohammad he was his usual friendly self. He told me again he had no desire for me to be relieved as his attorney. I looked over at the other defendants. They frowned at me. I felt more anger toward them than I did toward Mohammad. Once again, Mohammad had been manipulated, I told myself. His co-defendants had pressured him to write the letter, and maybe even their lawyers joined in. I fumed. My summation was an easy excuse for them. They could blame me if they were convicted.

WAS I right to be indignant or did Mohammad have a point? Legal ethicist Monroe Freedman dissected Mohammad's public disagreement with me in an article that appeared after the end of the trial.[1] Freedman posed a hypothetical. Assume it was tactically in Mohammad's interest for me to argue that he was not aware of the bomb plot and that he had been manipulated. And assume, although it may not be so, that I adopted this strategy contrary to Mohammad's instructions. Did I act ethically?

For my own part, I don't want to concede that I acted against Mohammad's instructions. I thought we had agreed on the general contours of the summation. I certainly did not think reversing the order of the arguments and shortening my attack on the physical evidence when the jury started to lose interest was a major departure from the strategy we had agreed on.

Nevertheless, Freedman's hypothetical raises issues that may become increasingly common in terrorism trials: defendants who want to protect conspiracy leaders and are willing to sacrifice themselves at trial to do so. What is the lawyer's ethical role? The answer to this question, Freedman believes, is to be found in the idea that at issue is not the lawyer's day in court but the defendant's. The client should be able to decide whether betraying his friends and religious colleagues is more important to him than avoiding prison: "And shouldn't the decision be the same if a husband refuses to exculpate himself by (truthfully) incriminating his wife? Or if a mother in a custody dispute chooses to forgo the tactical advantage of having her child testify, in order to avoid the trauma to the child?"[2]

Freedman uses sympathetic examples to support his conclusion that the defendant should have the final word on tactics. They are examples of parties in lawsuits choosing tactics that have the effect of sacrificing themselves to avoid harming third parties. But what if a defendant wants to dictate tactics to pursue goals that may not be so noble? Logically, the goals should not make a difference under Freeman's analysis. Thus, if a defendant wants the lawyer to call a child witness who would add little to the defense case but who would likely be traumatized, the lawyer is required to do so. Or if a defendant in a terrorism trial wants the lawyer to call a government informant who would add little to the defense case but who would be placed in physical danger, the lawyer is required to do so.

I do not believe that a defendant can or should dictate tactics. As we have seen, ABA model rule 1.2(a) says that a lawyer is required to abide by the client's decisions concerning the "objectives of representation." To me that means a lawyer must abide by a client's decision whether to go to trial to contest the charges, to plead guilty to avoid a long prison term, to cooperate with government authorities, and the like. Beyond that, it is the lawyer's call as to how best to achieve these objectives. The lawyer should consult with the client, but the lawyer has the final say as to tactics.

Freedman believes that this view undercuts one of the prime purposes of a trial, respecting the dignity and personal autonomy of the individual. He may be right. However, he ends his analysis by posing yet another hypothetical that seems to support my view that the lawyer should decide trial tactics:

> We'll never know whether Mohammed [*sic*] Salameh's charge against his lawyer was true. Imagine this scenario: *Lawyer:* Your only chance of getting off is to let the jury know that you were a dupe and that the real bad guy was your leader. *Client:* You're out of your mind. They'd probably kill me if I said that. *Lawyer:* Then what if we do it this way: I'll argue to the jury that you were just a dupe, and you'll tell your friends that you can't believe your ears, that I totally changed everything that you and I agreed on. *Client:* Sounds good to me. Let's do that.
>
> I don't know whether that's what happened, but it wouldn't be the first time that a lawyer took the heat for a client. Ironically, one of the reasons that lawyers have never been high in public esteem is that we do that job—taking the heat for the client—so well.[3]

For the record, Mohammad and I did not have an agreement that I would argue he was a dupe and that he would tell his friends he couldn't believe his ears. Yet the outcome was the same. Mohammad was not blamed for choosing tactics that might hurt his colleagues. I was blamed.

Making defense lawyers responsible for tactics is crucial in terrorism cases because the defendants might be members of militaristic organizations and under tremendous pressure not to say or do anything that will hurt the larger cause. If a defendant is deemed to have the final say, he will be more prone to pressure and intimidation from associates. If a lawyer is deemed to have the decisive voice, then he or she can take the blame for pursuing defenses that may help the defendant but harm his colleagues. That is probably a good thing, especially in terrorism cases.

CAMPRIELLO resumed his summation begun the previous Thursday. He was very eloquent, each phrase well turned, his tone finely nuanced, traversing a number of emotions effortlessly. He went out of his way to sound reasonable. He reviewed various mistakes the witnesses and the attorneys had made. He said I made a mistake by assuming that Yousef had access to money because he flew into the country on a first-class ticket. He excused these mistakes as reasonable human failings rather than signs of a conspiracy to wrongfully convict the four young men. The only reason Ajaj was on trial, he continued, was that Ajaj had the manuals and knew Yousef. But the manuals were in the hands of the government, and the association with Yousef was not enough to show that he had conspired with the man, especially since Ajaj was in jail at the time.

I had trouble concentrating on what Campriello was saying. Mohammad's denunciation gnawed at me. I tried to think rationally and stay calm, but I became increasingly agitated. From a purely strategic standpoint, Mohammad's complaint was a disaster. Judge Duffy instructed the jury every day to avoid reading the newspapers or watching television news, but there was always the danger that one or more jurors would disregard the order. If the jury got wind of the denunciation, the chances that they would seriously consider my summation arguments were nil. Why should the jury consider anything I said when my client was saying that he disagreed with me?

Campriello finished. The judge recessed the court for lunch. I pushed through the revolving doors into the noonday sun of Foley Square, where a mob of reporters clamored for me to comment about Mohammad's letter. If I said "no comment" again, I was afraid I would reinforce the notion that there had been a complete rupture between Mohammad and me. I decided to say something.

I chose my words carefully. "I stand by my summation a thousand per cent, and my client has reaffirmed his confidence in me as his lawyer." But I couldn't help feeling that I was reenacting Nixon's "I am not a crook" speech.

Back in my office, my boss Leonard laid into me for speaking to reporters.

"Why on earth did you say anything? You should've said 'no comment.' "

"Look, Leonard," I said, my voice rising, "people are saying I was bought off by the government. I had to say something!"

Leonard was right, of course. I should have said "no comment."

With Campriello's summation over, it was now Childers's turn to deliver the government's rebuttal summation, a normal practice in all federal criminal trials. Rebuttal summations are ordeals for defense lawyers. You must sit there as the prosecutor picks apart your summation, taking you to task for ignoring this item of evidence or that, criticizing you for trying to distract the jury, and you must sit mute, knowing that you won't be given the opportunity to respond.

For five months, Childers had been a model of lawyerly calm and stony unflappability. But stepping to the podium in front of the jury box after lunch, he disclosed a different side of his personality. Mixing indignation with sarcasm, he took us to task for accusing the government of twisting evidence to fit law enforcement theories.

"Over the last few days I've heard a lot of talk about victimization and things like that," Childers said in a hurt tone, "and who are the victims? Of course you'd think that maybe the thousand people who were killed—excuse me—thousand people who were injured and the six people who were killed at the World Trade Center might have been the victims, but no, it's the cruel government oppressing these four men, who have become the victims, the weight of the entire United States falling down upon four poor little gentlemen who have become the victims here."

Childers turned and looked at the defendants. "And, of course, who are the villains?" Childers asked sarcastically.

He then pointed to the government's table. "Anyone associated with that table are the villains. The assistant United States attorneys, the FBI agents," he said. "All these people got together obviously and conspired to suborn perjury and obstruct justice so you wouldn't be able to see what the truth was."

After these preliminaries, Childers attacked the summation arguments of each lawyer. He started with mine. He ripped into my assertion that Mohammad was a naive immigrant who was duped by the mastermind of the plot, Ramzi Yousef. "If Yousef was an 'evil genius,' Mohammad was his knowing assistant," Childers said.

He asked the jury to imagine the conversation Yousef and Mohammad would have had under my argument. He pointed out that a parking ticket receipt showed that they had gone to the World Trade Center days before the blast and stayed thirty minutes.

"I can see the scenario," said Childers. "You have Ramzi Yousef, the great manipulator, you have Mohammad Salameh, the innocent dupe. Ramzi Yousef says, 'hey, Mohammad, let's go over to the World Trade Center. Let's take a sight-seeing trip.' And Salameh goes, 'yeah, you know I've never been there. Let's go over.' They get into the parking garage; the parking attendant gives him the ticket. He puts it in his pocket and says, 'all right, Ramzi, where are we going? Windows on the World, the observation deck?' Ramzi goes, 'no, let's hang out here in the parking garage for a while. Hey, you think there is an X beam behind that wall we can blow out?'"

Childers continued in this vein, savaging the arguments of us all, until the end of the day. I listened, wishing I could respond but knowing I could not. What would be the point of responding anyway? Mohammad had disowned my theory. Feelings of helplessness mingled with anger. The case was in shambles.

22 Verdict

The clerk rose from his seat. "The court is about to charge the jury. Any spectator wishing to leave will do so now or remain seated until the completion of the court's charge. Marshal, lock the door."

This announcement, a ritual in all criminal cases, is intended to impress upon everyone in the courtroom the high seriousness of the court's instructions to the jury. No distractions will be tolerated. A court's final instructions are in marked contrast to the summations. Whereas summations tend to contain emotional appeals to the jury, the court's charge is supposed to be a cool and balanced explanation of the law the jury should apply when deciding the case. To guarantee balance, the law requires judges to give instructions on such principles as the presumption of innocence, reasonable doubt, and the defendant's right not to testify. Most judges deliver these instructions in a dry and pro forma manner that drains them of impact. Judge Duffy, by using homespun examples and simple, direct language, was one of those rare judges who tried to give these principles meaning.

From my standpoint, the two most important instructions were going to be those that dealt with the defendant's decision not to testify and the requirement that to be a member of a conspiracy one must knowingly advance its objectives—a requirement that went directly to my dupe defense.

On the right not to testify, most judges simply say that the decision cannot be considered as evidence against the defendant. The problem with this instruction is that it is counterintuitive and, without further explanation, likely to be disregarded by the jury. In everyday experience we expect that people who are falsely accused will want to defend themselves. When we hear someone charged with wrongdoing say "no comment," we assume the worst. To counteract our natural tendency to equate silence with guilt, stronger instructions are needed but are seldom given.

Judge Duffy gave these stronger instructions. He told the jury the usual about not holding the refusal to testify against them. But he took the unusual step of offering innocent explanations for why the defendants might not want to take the stand. "There are many, many reasons why a defendant might decide not to take the stand. He may feel that because of the strain and tension, he would not be a calm witness. He may feel that because English is not his native tongue, it might be difficult to express himself. He might be embarrassed by his lack of education. I don't know. He might be embarrassed by his inability to speak in front of a group of people. How would you feel if you were called upon to make a talk in front of a group of strangers? I guess that you would have a little clutch in your stomach just before you started. Everybody does. In fact, some people can't do it at all."

The judge turned to the main conspiracy charge. Since I had conceded the existence of the conspiracy in my summation, the central issue for Mohammad was whether he intentionally became a member of the conspiracy. My argument was that Mohammad was duped—he didn't know Yousef's illegal objectives and thus did not intentionally become a member of the conspiracy. Judge Duffy gave what I first thought to be a helpful instruction on this element. "To do something intentionally is to do it deliberately and purposefully. The defendant's acts must have been the product of the defendant's conscious objective, not the result of mistake or accident. The fact that the acts of a defendant without knowledge merely happened to further the purposes or objects of the conspiracy doesn't make that defendant a member. More is required under the law. What is necessary is that the defendant must have participated with knowledge of at least some of the basic aims and purposes of the conspiracy and with the intention of aiding in and accomplishing those unlawful ends." I was pleased with this instruction because it seemed to acknowledge my defense.

Turning to the question of how the jury should determine the intent of the defendants, Judge Duffy said that circumstantial evidence could often reveal more of a person's intent than can direct evidence. But suddenly, the judge's instructions started to hurt the defense. He improvised a folksy example that could hardly have been worse for us. "When you were a kid and you were in school, do you remember there was a bully? Some kid, he'd come along and he'd step on the toe of the guy beside him. The victim would yell. And the bully would look at the teacher and say, 'oh, it was a mistake. I didn't mean to do that. That was an accident.' Every other kid in the neighborhood knew that it was no mistake. Right?" I was alarmed. I had argued in my summation that Mohammad hadn't meant to blow up the Trade Center. "The direct evidence would be his declaration that it was a mistake and an accident. But by circumstantial evidence, ladies and gentlemen, you knew that it wasn't a mistake. It was him being a bully. You know, grownups are just big kids. We think the same way. You can conclude from circumstantial evidence what someone's intent or motive or knowledge was."

The problem with this charge was that the bully's guilt is assumed in the hypothetical's premise, and Judge Duffy simply instructed the jury on how to look for the evidence of that guilt. Since I was arguing that some of the circumstantial evidence pointed to Mohammad's innocence, the judge invited the jury to disregard it. John and I looked at each other and shook our heads.

Judge Duffy reviewed the elements of the other charges and prepared to conclude. If the jury wanted testimony read back, they could have it, he told them. No juror should enter into deliberations with such pride that he or she would be unwilling to change an opinion; nevertheless, don't change your opinion if to do so would do violence to your conscience, he told them.

Judge Duffy asked the lawyers to come to the side bar to place on the record any objections to the charge before he released the jury to begin its deliberations. John objected to the bully charge, and the judge overruled it.

THE jury began deliberating at four-thirty in the afternoon.

Waiting out a jury verdict is one of a lawyer's most stressful experiences. Of course, you tell yourself that the jury is deliberating your client's fate, but on some level you also believe that they are judging you. As you wait, you read all sorts of meaning into things such as how long the jury is taking and what notes if any they are sending to the judge. Did you persuade them? And if not, did you at least give them enough material during your cross-examination of witnesses and in your summation to put some of the government's evidence in doubt and to give the jury something to argue over?

A quick verdict, while it reduces the agony of waiting, leaves you with the distinct feeling that you failed miserably, that because your presentation was so unpersuasive the jury had little to talk about. A long wait, while perhaps allaying the concern that you didn't give the jury anything to argue about, gives rise to the hope of a not guilty verdict. The stakes seem to grow higher as the jury stays out longer, which creates another form of anxiety.

An hour into deliberations, the forewoman sent a note to the judge saying that the jury wanted to retire for the night. Judge Duffy didn't sequester them, and I was glad. Sequestration is almost always bad for the defense. If jurors are cut off from friends and family, compelled to spend their nights in a cheap motel under the gaze of U.S. marshals, they may feel pressured to decide the case quickly. When speed motivates deliberations, the defense arguments are often given short shrift, particularly in a complex case.

Deliberations resumed the next day. Although spectators are allowed to stay in the courtroom during deliberations, there were none. An eerie silence replaced the usual hubbub of the courtroom as the lawyers from both sides and the marshals mingled with each other waiting for the verdict. A winter wind howled outside, causing a whining sound through the windows. I noticed a marshal reading John Grisham's legal thriller *The Client*.

At about ten, the jury sent another note. They asked for a read-back of testimony from the early witnesses about the possible causes of the explosion, much of it consisting of the cross-examination by Ahmed that John and I had scorned. Was it possible the jury had any doubts that a bomb caused an explosion?

Later in the day, the jury asked for read-backs of testimony pertaining to Abouhalima. Did that mean they've already dispatched Mohammad? I wondered. It took some time for the lawyers to agree on what sections to read to the jury, and before we could collect all the sections the jury announced that they wanted to quit for the day. Because this was a Thursday, they would not be coming back until Monday. Saturday, February 26, 1994, would mark the one-year anniversary of the explosion, and Judge Duffy admonished the jury to be extra careful that day not to watch television.

Early Monday morning, I awoke at four, feeling terribly sad, scared, full of doubt. My head swirled with painful thoughts. Had I conceded too much in summation? Had I been driven subconsciously to provoke a rupture with Mohammad? And then an unbidden thought: what am I going to do when my parents are gone?

Deliberations resumed with the read-back of testimony about Abouhalima, including, as the jury requested, the direct and cross-examination of Ashref Moneeb, the young roommate of Mohammad whose green card had been seized by the FBI. I winced as the stenographer read outloud my inept cross-examination of the witness. The read-back concluded, the jury marshal took the jury back to the jury room. The slow-motion calm of the courtroom descended on us again.

Somehow, waiting for the verdict together, uncertain of our fates, the lawyers for both sides drew together for the first time in the case. The collegiality encouraged candor. Ahmed mused that Ayyad would probably claim on appeal that he was denied the effective assistance of counsel. "If Mr. Ayyad had listened to me, he would have had a real defense." I couldn't help wondering what that could be. One of the prosecutors assisting Childers confided that he was astonished that Ahmed had called no witnesses, not even a family member to refute the testimony of Ayyad's colleague identifying the defendant's voice on the Liberation Army tape. Now Ahmed began to read Grisham's *The Client*.

Abdellah studied the Koran. He remarked how difficult the case had been on him financially. His wife had cried again over the mounting bills just the night before. "Most rich clients with money hire white lawyers," he said without evident bitterness.

At 2:45, the jury asked for materials relating to Ajaj. I was sure they were going through the defendants one by one and had already voted to convict Mohammad. At 4:30, the jury decided to call it quits for the day and go home.

The next day, March 1, a crisis confronted us. During the morning rush hour, someone fired on a bus carrying Orthodox Jews across the Brooklyn Bridge. Reporters and television trucks were converging on lower Manhattan, and the incident would surely be the lead story on the six o'clock news. We feared the news would affect the jury's deliberations. The lawyers for both sides huddled with the judge to discuss how to respond to the development. The government wanted the jury sequestered but the defense lawyers resisted. After much debate, the judge reluctantly sided with us.

The deliberations continued. Childers was in a reflective mood. He spoke about his office, how it was largely staffed by young hotshots who wanted to work as prosecutors to burnish their resumes for cushy law firm jobs. Childers, who started out as a state prosecutor at the Brooklyn district attorney's office, had decided to make prosecution a career, eventually becoming a supervisor in the U.S. attorney's office. The case had taken a toll on his family life, and he expressed annoyance that he had had to agree to a demotion and take a pay cut because under internal rules supervisors cannot try cases.

Childers sang a song he composed to the tune of the old Allen Sherman comedy song "Hello Mudduh, Hello Fadduh." In the original song, a son writes a letter home to his parents from camp and describes his ordeals, and Allan Sherman sang it with a thick Bronx accent ("Hello Mudduh, hello Fadduh. Here I am at / Camp Granada. Now I don't want / That this should scare ya. But my bunk mate, has malaria"). In Childers's version, Ramzi Yousef, who referred to himself as Rashed, calls Ahmad Ajaj in prison: Childers began: "Hello Ahmad, This is Rashed. I'm so sorry, You got busted." The day ended with no indication that the jury was near a verdict.

The deliberations resumed the next day. Back in the courtroom, we watched a video of *Play Misty for Me*. The voice of Clint Eastwood boomed out in the empty, cavernous space. The day drew to a close. The forecast of a snowstorm the next day prompted the jury to ask for instructions in the event of inclement weather. Childers decided to ask Judge Duffy to keep the jury beyond the usual cutoff time, but it seemed he sensed it was a hopeless request. Pointing to one of the junior prosecutors assisting him, Childers said to the judge, "Mike has something to ask you." Mike demurred. Childers wound up his arm like a pitcher about to make throw. "I feel good about this one," and he asked the judge to keep the jury an extra hour. Judge Duffy shook his head. "Nice try."

However, the judge was clearly concerned about the Brooklyn Bridge incident and decided to put some pressure on the jury. "One way or the other, as far as inclement weather is concerned, if we're not working tomorrow, we're going to work on Friday. And if need be, my idea is to work on both Saturday and Sunday, also. So, file that away under 'incidental information,' so that you're aware of it."

On March 3, there was indeed a snowstorm, and court was canceled. At the office, John and I made half-hearted attempts to busy ourselves with small tasks, but we couldn't get our mind off deliberations. After lunch, Leonard asked us to come to his office.

He addressed me. "When the guilty verdict is announced, I'm sure the press will ask for your reaction. You can say the usual things, you know, that the jury has spoken and that you plan to appeal."

Guilty verdict? What a moronic, insensitive thing to say to me at such a time, I thought. Even if he believed that that was going to be the outcome, at least he could preserve the fiction that the case still hung in the balance. But I held my tongue. "Yes, I know," I said.

The next day, March 4, exactly a year after Mohammad was arrested and I was assigned to the case, the jury resumed deliberations under a bright winter sky. John and I were standing in the hallway outside the courtroom when, around noon, the clerk came out and told us that the jury had reached a verdict. They had done so after only four full days of deliberations.

We entered the courtroom, where reporters had already begun to fill up the seats. The prosecutors, however, were nowhere in sight. Several minutes passed. Suddenly, the judge's door opened. Out marched the judge. But the door remained opened, and a second later the prosecutors followed the judge into the courtroom. They were smiling. They had been with him. What was this shit?

Then it became clear. The judge had invited them back to the robing room to read them the jury's verdict and congratulate them. A tidal wave of anger swept over me. Duffy was treating the prosecutors as conquering heroes, when I and the other defense lawyers had presented equally valid, thoughtful cases.

The spectator section was now a sea of reporters. Marshals ringed the perimeter, as they had the first day of the case. Another row of them stood behind the defense table. The defendants were brought in, heads bowed.

The jury filed in. The courtroom fell to a hush. The judge asked the forewoman whether the jury had reached a verdict and she said, "We have, your Honor." Speaking in a clear, determined tone, she pronounced the word "guilty" thirty-eight times as the clerk of the court asked her the verdict on each of the charges against the four men.

All hell broke loose.

Ayyad shouted in Arabic, "Victory to Islam!" and the others joined in, chanting in unison. Mohammad rose from his seat, pointed to the jurors across the courtroom and yelled, "Injustice people!" I tried to pull him down but he resisted. "God is great!"

As marshals converged on the defendants, Ayyad's brother yelled from the back of the courtroom, "You are all fucking liars! My brother is innocent!"

"Arrest that man," Judge Duffy yelled.

The marshals dragged him away, while a much larger force hustled the defendants, still shouting slogans, out of the courtroom.

As the four were pushed out the back door of the courtroom, Mohammad turned toward the judge and cried in English, "Cheap people, cheap government!"

FOUR months after the verdict, in the middle of May, I was back in the courtroom for the sentencing. I greeted co-counsel, and we took our accustomed places at the defense table. Judge Duffy said, "We will now hear a statement from one of the victims."

A husky man in his thirties, looking uncomfortable in his suit, approached the lectern. When he introduced himself as Edward Smith, I recognized the name. His pregnant wife, Monica, had died in the blast, and I recalled the morgue picture of her. He evoked the memory of his dead wife and unborn baby in simple words. "Nobody could have ever prepared me for the feelings I was experiencing," he said, recalling the moment he learned his wife had died. "I had lost my wife, my best friend, my idol, and my son. I would never get the chance to tell Monica that I loved her."

As I listened to him, I experienced a strange sensation. Time seemed to telescope, and suddenly, I was very close to the human tragedy of the bombing. It was only three feet away from me in the form of an anguished young husband. I knew how I would feel if I had lost a loved one to terrorism. I wouldn't care if the terrorists received a fair trial.

"Injustice people!" Salameh shouts when the guilty verdicts are read. © Christine Cornell. Reprinted with permission.

Senior prosecutor Gilmore Childers, third from the left, speaking after the verdict at a news conference. Celebrating with him, from left, William Gavin, director of the New York regional FBI office; David Scott, first deputy police commissioner; Police Commissioner William Bratton; Henry DePippo, the other senior prosecutor; Romolo Imundi, director of federal marshals in New York; Mary Jo White, U.S. attorney for Manhattan; and Lev Dassin, a prosecutor. © AP/Wide World Photos. Reprinted with permission.

Mr. Smith finished. People were crying throughout the courtroom. I could barely hold back my own tears.

Judge Duffy turned to Mohammad and asked him if he had anything to say before the court pronounced the sentence. Mohammad said he did and addressed the court through an interpreter for fifteen minutes about the crimes of America. When he concluded, Judge Duffy called Mohammad a coward and a sneak. He calculated the sentence by figuring the life expectancy of each of the six people killed in the bombing and subtracting the number of years left in their lives. He then sentenced Mohammad to 240 years in prison, as he did the other defendants. Mohammad was silent when the marshals led him out of the courtroom. That was the last time I saw him.

23 Appeal

The final safeguard to ensure the integrity of the judicial process is appellate review. In theory, the courts of appeals examine trial proceedings and reverse decisions that may have resulted from violations of important statutory or constitutional rights. The judges who are assigned this role are a separate group of jurists who are removed from the passions of the trial process. Theoretically, this detachment gives them the objectivity to view a trial record dispassionately and to control the excesses of judge, jury, or prosecutor. This kind of review did not take place in Mohammad's case.

In its ninety-three-page opinion announced in 1998, the court of appeals affirmed the convictions.[1] The decision was most troubling because it never acknowledged the massive negative publicity that surrounded the case. This very factor demanded strong precautions by the judge and the prosecutor to keep the proceedings fair, an issue the court never touched upon. Instead, the court insisted that its review power was limited and sweepingly endorsed the actions of the judge and the prosecutors. The court recognized the potential unfairness of Judge Duffy's bully hypothetical but refused to overturn the verdict because other parts of the judge's charge were more balanced.

There were two other developments. Recall that prosecutors decided at the last minute not to call FBI chemist Fred Whitehurst after Whitehurst wrote that FBI agent David Williams pressured him and other scientists in the laboratory to slant their findings. Nevertheless, prosecutors called Williams, who then identified the contents of the bomb in direct contradiction to another government witness who said the contents could never be identified. In 1997, the Office of the Inspector General released a report into allegations of corruption in the FBI laboratory. The report found that large portions of David Williams's testimony were either downright false or completely unsupported by scientific evidence. Specifically, Williams had given invalid and misleading opinions when he testified that he could identify the type of bomb by looking at the destruction. He later admitted to inspector general investigators that he made the identification because he knew that agents had found urea nitrate at the storage locker. The report noted: "For Williams to identify the main charge as urea nitrate based on evidence that the defendants had or could make that compound is comparable to a firearms expert identifying the caliber of a spent bullet based on the mere fact that a suspect had a handgun of a particular caliber."[2]

Federal authorities arrested Ramzi Yousef in the Philippines in 1995 and flew him to New York to stand trial. He was tried with a co-defendant named Eyad Ismoil. Judge Duffy presided, and several members of the original prosecution team represented the government. Both defendants were convicted in December 1997. After arguing in the first trial that Mr. Moosh correctly identified Mohammad as the driver of the van on the morning of the explosion, prosecutors switched their theory. They did not call Mr. Moosh to testify. They now maintained that on the morning of the blast Ismoil—not Mohammad—drove the van to the World Trade Center.

Epilogue

After moving to Ann Arbor, I made frequent trips back to New York City. I always visited the World Trade Center. The repaired building had become more popular than ever. I felt drawn to it. It symbolized the resiliency of New York and the triumph of America over terrorism. In July 2001, two students and I ate lunch at Windows on the World on the 110th floor of the South Tower. I reminisced about my experiences trying the 1993 case. I can still recall the unique scent of the shop-filled concourse that day after lunch: the mingled aromas of perfume, coffee, pastries, and the metallic, earthy smell emanating from the nearby subway entrances.

After the initial shock of seeing the towers collapsing on television on the morning of September 11, my next reaction was anger. I hated Mohammad. Erased from my thoughts was the young man I had gotten to know and even to like during the time we had spent together. A new image replaced the old one, that of a hardened, brutal killer. This is what he would have done if he had had his way, I thought. This was his idea of justice. I recalled the police officer's testimony in the 1993 trial about rescuing a small child from a trapped elevator and how she had clung to his neck.

I found myself sympathizing with those who say that terrorism should be fought not by the criminal justice system but by the military. Military authorities could hold suspects indefinitely and subject them to intensive interrogation, after which a military commission rather than a civilian court would try them. This approach would give the government the means to prevent future terrorist attacks and protect its intelligence sources. Law is a tool to serve the purposes of our officials in this vital work, the argument goes, certainly not one to curtail the well-intentioned uses of power to protect the country.

On further reflection, I believe the military approach is not the right solution.

Military tribunals cannot deliver an essential ingredient of fairness—neutrality. There is no process similar to jury voir dire to eliminate biased officers from judging the accused. Unlike the typical jury, whose members reflect a diversity of views, military judges are drawn from the military organization, and they inevitably see their judging role in the context of prosecuting a war. They are encouraged to prejudge—to categorize people as the enemy too quickly and to assume the worst about a suspect too readily. Moreover, their judgment is not subject to judicial review.

Impartiality is important not only to the achievement of justice in particular cases, but also to the attainment of legality throughout the whole world. If America gives up on that value, there is bound to be a backlash, both at home and abroad. Many of the subjects might be innocent people, which would be morally repugnant. Ordinary Americans will be encouraged to follow in the footsteps of military judges, stereotyping their immigrant neighbors and viewing them suspiciously through war-tinted glasses. Another problem will be maintaining cooperation with America's European allies. They may be guilty of lapses, but European governments take international treaties guaranteeing the impartial administration of justice seriously.[1] Moreover, repressive regimes will feel they have a license to act ruthlessly against perceived enemies, and they will point to the U.S. as an example.

It especially seems premature to give up on the criminal justice system when there is no evidence that the system is unable to handle terrorism cases. The 1993 Trade Center trial was swift, and it did not disclose government secrets. While I believe the trial was unfair, the fault was not that the system lacked safeguards. Rather, the participants failed to use them. Jury trials are not perfect. There's considerable evidence that jurors are not always smart decision makers, that they don't always follow instructions and don't always abide by their oaths.[2] Nevertheless, the jury trial system is premised on the idea of impartiality, a concept alien to military tribunals, which lack any safeguards for insuring it.

The Boston Massacre of 1770 was condemned by the American media as a "bloody butchery" and a symbol of British tyranny. Paul Revere and others embarked on a campaign to inflame the citizenry's emotions, demonizing the British and always casting the revolutionaries in the most virtuous light.[3] There was popular clamor for vengeance. John Adams, who would later become the second president of the United States, insisted that the soldiers receive a fair trial. He and a colleague undertook to defend the unpopular men. There were no military judges, no incommunicado detention of the defendants, no degrading treatment or intensive interrogation. The defense lawyers were free to cross-examine the prosecution's witnesses and to call their own. The jury convicted two of the accused and aquitted the rest.

In his closing argument to the jury, Adams stated: "Facts are stubborn things; and whatever may be our wishes, our inclinations, or the dictates of our passions, they cannot alter the state of facts and evidence. Nor is the law less stable than the fact. . . . To your candor and justice, I submit the prisoners and their cause."[4]

The best weapon we have against terrorists is not our passions. It is the rule of law.

Notes

Chapter 1. My Appointment

1. U.S. Const. amend. VIII.
2. See 18 U.S.C. § 3142(e), (f) (2000).

Chapter 2. The Right to a Fair Trial

1. *Strickland v. Washington*, 466 U.S. 668, 685 (1984).
2. Stephan Landsman, "When Justice Fails," *Michigan Law Review* 84 (1986): 824, 833.
3. Samuel R. Gross, "Lost Lives: Miscarriages of Justice in Capital Cases," *Law and Contemporary Problems* (autumn 1998): 125.
4. Alison Mitchell, "Suspect in Bombing Is Linked to Sect with a Violent Voice," *New York Times*, March 5, 1993, A1.
5. Jim McGee, "Trade Center Probe Is Far from Done," *Washington Post*, March 7, 1993, A1.
6. Lance Morrow, "In the Name of God," *Time*, March 15, 1993, 24.
7. Gaylord Shaw, "Anti-Terrorism Plan Backed," *Newsday*, March 6, 1993, 77.
8. Bethany Kandel and Bruce Frankel, "Bomb Probe Could Take 'Years,'" *USA Today*, March 8, 1993, 3A.

Chapter 3. "We Try Cases in the Courtroom"

1. See 18 U.S.C. § 3161(c)(1).
2. Because Judge Duffy entered the gag order against me and the other lawyers personally and threatened to fine us in our individual capacities, I thought it prudent to have a lawyer represent me rather than to represent myself, especially when an acknowledged First Amendment expert volunteered.
3. *Gentile v. State Bar of Nevada*, 501 U.S. 1030, 1038 (1990).
4. *United States v. Salameh*, 992 F.2d 445, 446 (2d Cir. 1993).

Chapter 4. Discovery

1. See *Weatherford v. Bursey*, 429 U.S. 545, 559 (1977).
2. *Brady v. Maryland*, 373 U.S. 83, 87 (1963).
3. See Fed. R. Crim. P. 16(a).
4. *Roviaro v. United States*, 353 U.S. 53, 59 (1957).
5. Ibid., 60–65.
6. *United States v. Gallo*, 654 F.Supp. 463 (E.D.N.Y. 1987), *order vacated, In re United States*, 834 F.2d 283 (2d Cir. 1987).
7. *Roviaro v. United States*, 353 U.S. 53 (1957).
8. *United States v. Salameh*, 1993 WL 168568 (S.D.N.Y. 1993).

Chapter 5. Strategy

1. See 18 U.S.C. §§ 3591–98 (1994).
2. *United States v. Salameh*, 152 F.3d 88, 145 (2d Cir. 1998).
3. A notable example was the indictment against Zacarias Moussaoui, the so-called twentieth highjacker in the September 11 attacks. The first count was a catchall conspiracy charge similar to the one found in the 1993 World Trade Center indictment. The indictment alleged that he was a member of a conspiracy to kill persons within the United States. The destruction of the World Trade Center was one of 112 overt acts listed.
4. See *Coolidge v. New Hampshire*, 403 U.S. 443, 450 (1971).
5. *Johnson v. United States*, 333 U.S. 10, 13–14 (1948).
6. See *Franks v. Delaware*, 438 U.S. 154 (1978).
7. The government indicted Yasin. He remains a fugitive. He is believed to be alive and living in Iraq.
8. See, e.g., Jan Mills Spaeth, "Swearing with Crossed Fingers: Juror Honesty and Voir Dire," *Arizona Attorney*, January 2001, 39.

Chapter 6. "Can You Be Fair and Impartial?"

1. *United States v. Salameh*, 1993 WL 364486 (S.D.N.Y.).
2. See *Chandler v. Florida*, 449 U.S. 560, 574 (1981).
3. The Supreme Court proscribed race-based peremptory challenges in *Batson v. Kentucky*, 476 U.S. 80 (1986), and gender-based peremptory challenges in *J.E.B. v. Alabama ex rel. T.B.*, 511 U.S. 127 (1994).

Chapter 8. Relevance and Prejudice

1. Gross, "Lost Lives," 148.
2. Federal Rule of Evidence 401 states, "'Relevant evidence' means evidence having any tendency to make the existence of any fact that is of consequence to the determination of the action more probable or less probable than it would be without the evidence."

3. Federal Rule of Evidence 403 states: "Although relevant, evidence may be excluded if its probative value is substantially outweighed by the danger of unfair prejudice, confusion of the issues, or misleading the jury, or by considerations of undue delay, waste of time, or needless presentation of cumulative evidence."

4. See *Richardson v. Marsh*, 481 U.S. 200, 210 (1987).

5. The discussion of the victims relies on the reporting of Jim Dwyer with David Kocieniewski, Deidre Murphy, and Peg Tyre, *Two Seconds under the World* (New York: Ballantine, 1994).

Chapter 9. "How Are You Going to Feel?"

1. Lon Fuller, "The Adversary System," in *Talks on American Law*, ed. H. Berman (New York: Vintage Books, 1961), 40.

2. Ibid., 37.

3. Ibid.

4. See, e.g., *Miranda v. Arizona*, 384 U.S. 436 (1966) (the right to the presence of an attorney during custodial police interrogations); *United States v. Wade*, 388 U.S. 218 (1967) (the right to be represented by counsel during post-indictment identification procedures, such as lineups); and *Brady v. Maryland*, 373 U.S. 83 (1963) (the right to obtain from the government evidence favorable to the accused).

5. See *Brown v. Miss.*, 297 U.S. 278, 286–87 (1936).

6. *Blackburn v. Alabama*, 361 U.S. 199, 206–207 (1960).

Chapter 10. Cross-Examination

1. Federal Rule of Evidence 801(c) defines hearsay as "a statement, other than one made by the declarant while testifying at the trial or hearing, offered in evidence to prove the truth of the matter asserted."

Chapter 12. "A Person like This One"

1. Richard Bernstein, "Witness Fails to Identify Blast Defendants," *New York Times*, December 8, 1993, B1.

Chapter 15. A Christmas Visit

1. Haruki Murakami, *Underground* (New York: Vintage Books, 2001).

2. Ibid., 364.

Chapter 16. "I'm Fairly Certain He Did It"

1. Fed. R. Crim. P. 11(d)(f); Fed. R. Evid. 410.

2. See *U.S. v. Mezzanatto*, 513 U.S. 196, 210 (1995).

3. Title 28 U.S.C. § 455(a) states: "Any justice, judge, or magistrate of the United States shall disqualify himself in any proceeding in which his impartiality might reasonably be questioned."

4. See 28 C.F.R. § 501.3(d). The rule permits the attorney general, without a prior court order, to authorize the monitoring of all communications between a person in federal custody and that person's lawyer whenever the attorney general has "reasonable suspicion" to believe that a person "may use communications with attorneys or their agents to further or facilitate acts of terrorism."

Chapter 17. "It Was Misleading"

1. *Napue v. Illinois*, 360 U.S. 264, 269 (1959).
2. FBI laboratory home page, http://www.fbi.gov/hq/lab/labhome.htm.

Chapter 19. "Do Not Cry"

1. See Wayne R. Lafave, Jerold H. Israel, and Nancy King, *Criminal Procedure*, 3d ed. (St. Paul: West Group, 2000), § 8.14(b).

Chapter 20. Summations

1. See ABA model rule 1.2(a).

Chapter 21. "I Could Not Believe My Ears"

1. Monroe Freedman, "Whose Case Is It, Anyway," *Texas Lawyer*, May 9, 1994, 18.
2. Ibid.
3. Ibid.

Chapter 23. Appeal

1. *United States v. Salameh*, 152 F.3d 88 (2d Cir. 1998).
2. See Michael R. Bromwich, Inspector General, *The FBI Laboratory: An Investigation into Laboratory Practices and Alleged Misconduct in Explosives-Related and Other Cases*, April 1997, http://www.usdoj.gov/oig/fbilab1/04wtc97.htm.

Epilogue

1. Article 6 of the European Convention on Human Rights guarantees the right to a "fair and public hearing within a reasonable time by an independent and impartial tribunal established by law."

2. A good example of the scholarship criticizing the jury system is Jerome Frank, *Courts on Trial* (Princeton, N.J.: Princeton University Press, 1976).

3. David McCullough, *John Adams* (New York: Touchstone, 2002), 65–68.

4. Doug Linder, Boston Massacre trial page, http://www.law.umkc.edu/faculty/projects/ftrials/bostonmassacre/adamssummation.html.

Suggested Reading

Allen, Francis A. *The Habits of Legality: Criminal Justice and the Rule of Law.* New York: Oxford University Press, 1996. Allen argues that even in times of crisis the government must be bound and limited by rules and that sanctions against individuals for breaking the rules must be imposed only by impartial and independent courts.

Arendt, Hannah. *Eichmann in Jerusalem: A Report on the Banality of Evil.* New York: Penguin Books, 1992. Arendt examines the problem of rendering individualized justice to people accused of crimes against humanity.

Aussaresses, Paul. *The Battle of the Casbah: Terrorism and Counter-Terrorism in Algeria 1955–1957.* Translated by Robert L. Miller. New York: Enigma Books, 2002. A retired general who served in the French army during the Algerian war defends his use of extrajudicial means—including torture—to prevent terrorism.

Avrich, Paul. *The Haymarket Tragedy.* Princeton: Princeton University Press, 1986. The 1886 bombing trial of Chicago anarchists foreshadowed the difficulty of giving accused terrorists a fair trial.

Dershowitz, Alan M. *Why Terrorism Works: Understanding the Threat, Responding to the Challenge.* New Haven: Yale University Press, 2002. A law professor provides a provocative overview of some of the moral and practical questions relating to America's "war on terror," particularly regarding homeland security.

Landsman, Stephan A., ed. *American Bar Association Section of Litigation Readings on Adversarial Justice: The American Approach to Adjudication.* St. Paul, Minn.: West Group, 1992. Essays and debates on the adversary system help readers compare civilian trials for accused terrorists with their most likely replacements, military tribunals.

Lewis, Anthony. *Gideon's Trumpet.* New York: Vintage Books, 1989. This dramatic history of the right to counsel is one of the best introductions to the American criminal justice system.

Murakami, Haruki. *Underground.* New York: Vintage Books, 2001. The people responsible for the 1995 terrorist attack on Tokyo's subway system were motivated by disturbingly familiar emotions.

Rehnquist, William H. *All the Laws but One: Civil Liberties in Wartime*. New York: Vintage Books, 2000. The Chief Justice of the United States reviews prominent cases in which civilians have been tried by military tribunals, from President Lincoln's suspension of habeas corpus to the imposition of martial law in Hawaii during World War II.

Index